The Hub Shootout: San Diego's Unbelievable Four-hour Firefight

John Culea

Cover: The image is from the first moments of the Hub shootout. (Courtesy: The Brown family)

Also by John Culea:
Light the Night
Best Moves
In the Air * On the Air
Air Apparent
The Trail through Mohawk
The Rails through Mohawk
The Highway through Mohawk
Target Tombstone
Miner Leaguer
SanDiegoLand
Expo 2 Padres 1
Infamy to Injustice: Liberty's Shame

October 25, 2018
John Culea
9019 Stargaze Avenue
San Diego, CA 92129
john.culea@gmail.com

The Hub Shootout:
San Diego's Unbelievable
Four-hour Firefight

John Culea

4

To Patti

CONTENTS

The Hub Shootout:
San Diego's Unbelievable
Four-hour Firefight

John Culea

8

Forward

My father, Allen D. Brown was a remarkable man. On April 8, 1965, his actions made him a larger-than-life legend for the San Diego Police Department. *The Hub Shootout: San Diego's Unbelievable Four-hour Firefight* is the story of that day and how my father distinguished himself with bravery above and beyond the call of duty.

The book also shows how the police department changed the way it would respond to future emergencies and also the impact the case had on California's judicial system.

I know that the San Diego County law enforcement community will be thankful this book has been written as it shows with dramatic and new details what police faced on that rainy day at Fifth and F in downtown San Diego. While other police officers had tactical supervision how the incident was handled, my father was the "go-to" guy who eventually brought down the man who after murdering a kind and innocent pawnshop manager was holed up inside and with an arsenal of weapons and ammunition held off police for four hours.

On that day, I was at the police academy eight blocks west from the shootout learning how to become a cop. My father's actions showed me what it took to serve and protect in the highest traditions of the police department.

Whatever success I have achieved in life began with the fundamentals my father taught and lived out on a daily basis. I am honored to share my thoughts in loving and grateful memory of my father, Lieutenant Allen D. Brown.

Frank A. Brown
Retired San Diego County Superior Court Judge

Preface

This book is based on an event that happened April 8, 1965 in San Diego, California. Specific details of the incident differed widely not only immediately after the shootout but in the weeks, months and years that followed. While the author used oral, written and visual accounts in an attempt to accurately report what occurred, he has taken liberty to speculate on what might have been the thoughts, words and actions of people who were caught in the middle of the biggest and longest shootout in San Diego Police Department history.

The case also had profound impacts on California's judicial system and how the San Diego Police Department responds to tactical confrontations today.

Many of the images in the book are taken from KGTV and KFMB-TV video that is part of a 2010 DVD, "Hub Loans Shooting Incident April 8, 1965." The video is on auto-play at the San Diego Police Museum, 4710 College Avenue, San Diego, California 92115. The author is grateful to the San Diego Police Historical Association, KGTV and KFMB-TV for granting the right to use the compelling visual record.

Just like all American institutions, our nation's police departments have changed over the years. They have modernized and recognized the need to adjust to societal evolution. Yet at the core, the men and women who protect and serve have not wavered in their fundamental fight against crime and lawlessness and remain a symbol of what makes our nation great. I profoundly admire these brave officers and hope this book serves as a tribute to their courage and professionalism.

And finally, something that was unexpected. While researching and writing the book, I was able to bring together several members of the San Diego Police Department who had lost touch, in some cases for several decades with old friends and partners. Their joy made me feel really good.

Chapter 1
The People

On a rainy Thursday morning, April 8, 1965, 61-year-old Louis Richards unlocked the front door of the Hub Loans & Jewelry Company at the southeast corner of Fifth Avenue and F Street in downtown San Diego. Richards, five feet five inches tall and a pudgy 170 pounds, was the store's sales and credit manager. He moved to San Diego from Israel 30 years earlier and had worked at the Hub for 22 years. It would be the last day of his life.

Louis Richards
(Courtesy San Diego Police Museum)

Hub Loans & Jewelry Company, a partnership consisting of Sam Zemen and the estate of Max Zeman at 771 Fifth Avenue also was a popular pawnshop with an arsenal of weapons and ammunition for sale. The store was below the five-story William Penn Hotel, then a seedy residence in the heart of San Diego's downtown Gaslamp Quarter. The area, littered with tattoo parlors, dank bars, penny arcades, peep shows and strip joints was a hangout for hard luck cases and sailors on liberty. Police officers say they knew several bars were controlled by organized crime that supplied jukeboxes and bar supplies.

As the Hub's credit manager, Richards was all too familiar with desperate men and women needing money. He had heard every sob story and tale of woe a hundred times. Constantly dealing with despairing souls might harden a person, but somehow Richards maintained a bright outlook, so much so, that other pawnbrokers in the district dubbed him "Mr. Sunshine." Down-and-outers who lived on the streets knew him for his generosity. Even so, Richards was a veteran businessman and understood that while the circumstances varied, there was one constant he could count on; people always thought what they were either selling or exchanging for a loan was more valuable than what Richards was going to give them. But since there was no credit check and no other ready cash source for customers, the Hub's policy was "take it or leave it." More often than not, most people surrendered what they brought in, took what money was offered and left. On this day Louis Richards' life would be taken.

* * * * *

At the same time Richards was opening the Hub, 28-year-old Robert Page Anderson was on a bus headed toward downtown. Five-feet-five inches tall and weighing not much more than 100 pounds, he wore a small goatee and kept his hair short while concealing a hair-trigger temper. Years later, Anderson was quoted as saying, "I wish I never got off that bus."

Robert Anderson
(Courtesy San Diego Police Museum)

(Courtesy San Diego Police Museum and San Diego
History Center)

    Having scraped together a few coins for bus fare, the
part-time janitor and unemployed window washer with a
history of drug abuse, petty crimes and scuffles with the
law was in a familiar dilemma. He was nearly broke and
with less than $2, Anderson had a diamond ring in his
pocket he hoped would bring some cash. Still owing $60
on a conditional sales contract, to his dismay he would
soon realize the ring was only going to get him about $10
cash.
    Anderson, born on January 4, 1937, had lived his life
in obscurity, overlooked and underachieving in a San
Diego black neighborhood. He neither understood nor
trusted white people. At the age of five after being
abandoned by his parents, his aging grandmother, Mrs.
Mattie Anderson tried to raise him at 3211 Webster Street.

On this day he was on probation after serving six months in jail for marijuana possession. It was the latest in a series of offenses that included stabbing another boy when he was 14 and attacking an inmate at a correctional facility with a shovel. Little else is known of his juvenile years because his records were inadvertently destroyed.

* * * * *

Not too far away from the Hub, 52-year-old Robert Crandall, a newspaper editor for the *Independent* was preparing for another day of battle with the giant Copley-owned rivals, the morning *San Diego Union* and the *San Diego Evening Tribune.*

Robert Crandall
(Courtesy Brown family)

Crandall, a native of Chicago had studied at Northwestern University and was a veteran journalist with previous stints at small newspapers in Colorado, Nevada and California before becoming the *Independent's* editor four years earlier.

    Normally, his thoughts would have been on the near impossible task of trying to beat the city's two powerful newspapers, but Crandall's personal life was falling apart. Having a history of minor heart attacks, the stress on him now was nearly unbearable because an hour earlier, he had learned an interlocutory divorce decree had been granted to his wife, Willie who lived in Sacramento. The charge: mental cruelty. The court judgment would not be final until a judge determined if enough time had passed to see if the interim decision was working. For Crandall, it wouldn't matter. An hour after learning the news, Robert Crandall would be dead.

* * * * *

    Also at the Hub that morning was 63-year-old Theodore "Ted" Swienty who had worked at the Hub for two years. An Army Private in World War I, he knew about firearms and usually helped customers who wanted to buy guns and ammunition. He was also a man who twice in the past had cheated death.

Ted Swienty
(Courtesy KFMB-TV and San Diego Police Museum)

While working as a cook on the tuna clipper Mary Barbara off the Galapagos Islands, Swienty, a veteran of the tuna fleet was swept overboard. He suffered deep shark bites on his left foot and right leg before being pulled to safety.

He was hospitalized for seven months but doctors were able to save both his legs. Later a jury awarded him $40,000 in damages from the National Marine Terminal, Inc., operator of the boat.

Then in January 1959, again while on the Mary Barbara off the coast of Mexico, a high wave knocked him overboard, supposedly when the tuna boat made a sudden turn. He escaped from a school of sharks after being bitten several times and was rescued by crew members who put a skiff overboard and hauled him out of the water before he was eaten alive. Swienty said he saved his life by lying on top of a life ring thrown to him and playing "possum" on the theory sharks are less likely to hit a still form in the water. He would also play "possum" on April 8, 1965, but nothing he experienced in the "War to End All Wars" or in shark-infested waters would come close to what he was about to face.

* * * * *

Eight blocks west from the Hub on Market Street, San Diego Police Sergeant Allen Brown was reviewing reports of officers he commanded in a squad room at police headquarters. Joe Stone in the *San Diego Union* wrote that Brown was working on an accident report in which a patrolman had done $5 worth of damage to a patrol car.

It was 10:12 A.M. and after being there since three in the morning, Brown was scheduled to get off work when he heard the report that there was a shooting at a downtown pawnshop. He checked with the patrol captain and was sent immediately to the scene.

Allen D. Brown
(Courtesy San Diego Police Museum)

Brown had been a police officer for 17 years and was considered a "cop's cop." A legend among officers, Brown would go to a fried chicken restaurant in Pacific Beach at the end of the night to pick up unsold chicken and then give it to other police officers. He got in trouble for doing that, but saying it was the right thing to do for his men, he didn't stop.

Rookie officer Allen D. Brown in 5th Academy Class
photo 1948, courtesy The Informant, October 1980
Sergeant Allen Brown (far left standing) in a 1962 photo,
courtesy San Diego Police Museum.

Allen Brown was born January 3, 1920 in the
Philippines, where his father, an Army colonel was
stationed. He moved to San Diego in 1943 and went to
work building airplanes for the war at Consolidated Vultee
Aircraft Corporation's plant near Lindbergh Field not far
from where Lindbergh's "Spirit of St. Louis" had been
designed, built and tested in 1927.

Even though Brown had an occupational deferment
because of his defense-related job, the 24-year-old Brown
enlisted in the Army in 1944. He became a paratrooper and
reached the rank of second lieutenant seeing action in
Okinawa and was part of the Japan occupation forces.

On the afternoon of April 8, 1965, Sergeant Brown
would be hailed as a hero.

* * * * *

The officer in charge of the scene outside the Hub on
April 8, 1965 was 48-year-old Inspector Wayne Colburn
who had been with the San Diego Police Department for
22 years. His service with the SDPD was interrupted
during the Korean War when he was recalled to active
duty in the Marine Corps.

Wayne Colburn
(Courtesy KGTV, KFMB-TV and San Diego Police
Museum)

    Returning to the police force in 1951, Colburn was promoted to Sergeant. In the years that followed, he rose in the ranks to Lieutenant, Captain and Inspector. In 1966 he retired from the San Diego Police Department and in 1968 was appointed by President Lyndon Johnson to head the United States Marshals Service for the newly formed Southern District of California.

    In 1970, the U.S. Attorney General selected Colburn to become Director of the United States Marshals Service. Three years later, he was in command of a standoff involving 300 militant Native American Indians at Wounded Knee, South Dakota. It lasted 71days and ended with the deaths of two Indians.

    Eight years earlier at the Hub standoff, Colburn used bullets and a bullhorn to no avail.

* * * * *

    Wesley Sharp was the San Diego Chief of Police on April 8, 1965.

Wesley Sharp 1931   (Courtesy San Diego Police
(Courtesy S.D.P.O.A)   Museum)

    Three years earlier, at the age of 64, thinking he was too old for the job, the bespectacled 34-year veteran of the force reluctantly took the top spot. His tenure was in the middle of great civil unrest across the nation with racial tensions at the breaking point and growing protests against the Viet Nam War. Concerned about his patrolmen's safety, Sharp ordered uniformed officers below the rank of lieutenant to wear safety helmets at all times when on duty and that chinstraps be buckled. Those caught violating the order got a two-day suspension without pay.

Sharp's first assignment in the early Depression years of 1931 was downtown foot patrol. Four months later he was promoted to detective and never had to wear a police uniform again.

* * * * *

On April 8, 1965, Navy Gunner's Mate Third Class Frank W. Morales was on day watch shore patrol duty on his way to downtown San Diego.

(Courtesy KGTV and San Diego Police Museum)
He was likely thankful not having to deal with the nighttime challenge of keeping peace among drunken sailors on liberty and had often responded to Navy reports of fistfights on the streets near the Hub. However, on this day the petty officer heard over his short-wave radio that police were looking for a gunner's mate who knew how to use hand grenades. He volunteered and was told to drive directly to Fifth and F and report to the police.

Frank Morales' actions in the next four hours would earn him the Navy and Marine Corps Medal for heroism.

* * * * *

Without knowing it, all of the major players in the Hub shootout were in place.

Chapter 2
The City

Compared with now, you would have had difficulty recognizing the city of San Diego and surrounding San Diego County in 1965. The city had a population of about 600,000, the county around one million. In 2018 those numbers had tripled. However, the change involved much more than people.

In 1965, in order to reach Coronado from San Diego, you still had to take a ferry. A one-way ride cost 45¢. For years, efforts to build a bridge were rejected by voters, largely because the Navy feared attack or an earthquake could collapse a bridge and trap ships stationed at Naval Station San Diego. In 1935, Navy brass at the naval air station at North Island said if a bridge were built to cross the bay, then the Navy would leave San Diego. But in 1964, the Navy gave its blessing for a bridge if there were at least 200 feet clearance for ships to pass underneath it.

Work proceeded but the bridge would not open until 1969. In April 1965, only pilings could be seen sticking out of the water in San Diego Bay and the start of building the span was still two years away.

Elsewhere in 1965, there were plans to construct and open a multi-purpose sports stadium in Mission Valley in 1968 that would be the new home for the San Diego Chargers who were playing their games at Balboa Stadium south of Balboa Park.

In 1965, the San Diego Padres were a Pacific Coast League farm club of the Cincinnati Reds, one of twelve teams in an odd set-up that was hardly pacific coast. Indianapolis, Salt Lake City, Oklahoma City, Denver and the Arkansas Travelers in Little Rock were among PCL franchises.

The Padres played their games at Westgate Park in Mission Valley, a neat little ballpark that would be torn down in 1969. The minor league Padres with stars like Tommy Helms and Lee May would relocate to Eugene in 1968 a year after San Diego was awarded a National League expansion team.

In April 1965, unlike beautiful Westgate Park, the area around the Hub in San Diego was a run down mess. In some ways the Gaslamp Quarter was timeless in its connection to the past. Nearby was where Wyatt Earp ran three gambling halls in the 1880's and spent seven years four blocks away from the grit and grime as a guest of the Grand Horton Hotel on F Street. It was built in 1887 as a luxury hotel with a design based on the Innsbruck Inn in Vienna, Austria. The construction was part of a building boom after San Diego's first transcontinental railroad connection two years earlier.

Just like the days of the Wild West, in 1965 the Hub was in a zone of poverty, poor housing, shootings, prostitution, muggings, street fights and violent crime.

Transformation was years away. People dreamed and talked about making the area a national and historic district that would bring upper middle-class tourists and suburban residents to downtown San Diego. But in April 1965, there was no denying the Gaslamp Quarter was an eyesore that had run out of gas.

The City of San Diego in 1965 was also embroiled in scandal. Its mayor, Frank Curran would be forced out of office for taking bribes from a taxi company in exchange for approving higher rates.

Four miles from downtown San Diego and the Hub, two military facilities in 1965 were ramping up the number of Navy and Marine Corps personnel called into service to feed the Viet Nam War.

The Naval Training Center's boot camp recruit population surged to 18,000 while the nearby Marine Corps Recruit Depot and Camp Pendleton to the north were turning out thousands of Marines, who would soon find themselves in firefights in South Viet Nam's hamlets and cities.

On April 8, 1965, San Diegans were reading newspaper coverage of President Lyndon Johnson's major foreign policy speech the night before. Mr. Johnson said the United States was ready for "unconditional discussions" of a Viet Nam peace. But he also restated at the same time a no-retreat position, while opening the door wider to possible negotiations. In the years to come, the President would not seek re-election and never saw a glimmer of peace. Instead, the words he spoke on April 7 that came true were "we must be prepared for a long continued conflict."

While the battles in the hamlets and cities of South Viet Nam were 13,000 miles to the west, another firefight was about to erupt in San Diego's Gaslamp Quarter, a standoff the San Diego Police Department had never faced before.

Chapter 3
The Confrontation

The morning of April 8, 1965, Robert Page Anderson was on a bus near Fifth Avenue and F Street in San Diego. The driver probably hadn't greeted him when he got on. This was not unusual. Anderson was used to people looking through him as if he were invisible. Anderson had asked for a transfer and put it in his pocket. As the bus continued its route, Anderson may have admired the way the driver was able to maneuver the 40-foot, 10-ton bus through downtown San Diego. From his seat at the front of the bus, Anderson watched the driver and since he didn't have a job, perhaps wondered if he could handle one of the city buses. But being as short as he was, he would have been challenged to reach the pedals.

There are several accounts of what was about to happen. One version had Anderson carrying a diamond ring in his pocket that he hoped he could pawn for $100. Considering he had less than two dollars to his name, it's uncertain why he had the ring and what he was going to do with it. Since it later was made known he was paying for the ring with monthly payments, it wasn't stolen. Was it a personal ring or an engagement ring he planned to give to a girlfriend? We'll never know. Whatever, the reason, Anderson had decided to get as much as he could for the ring at the Hub pawnshop.

Months later, Anderson would say he had gone downtown that day to see a movie. Jutta Biggins, widow of attorney James. D. Biggins, Jr. who later would defend Anderson verified the story in a 2018 interview.

James and Jutta Biggins
(Courtesy Jutta Biggins)

Another version was that Anderson wanted to buy a suitcase. He also would say that he had bought a Derringer pistol in another pawnshop. Realizing he was convicted in 1962 on a narcotics violation, Anderson would say he knew it was illegal for an ex-convict to possess firearms, but he considered the Derringer more of an antique than a weapon.

Whatever the true story was, while on the bus Anderson saw his destination ahead and reached above his head and pulled a bus cord that let out a loud *ding*.

When the bus came to Anderson's stop, he stood and waited for the door to open. As it did, once again, the driver probably ignored the little man as he prepared to get off. *Screw him*, Anderson may have thought and walked down the steps.

Anderson likely chided himself for not wearing a jacket to protect him from the rain that steadily fell. He would ater say the movie he wanted to see did not start until 2 P.M. so he walked by the Hub store and wondered whether he could get a "good deal" by exchanging his diamond ring for a rifle.

Outside the pawnshop, Anderson saw an older man washing a large window that fronted the store. It was Ted Swienty who had arrived at the store at 8:15 that morning.

Opening the door, Anderson walked into the pawnshop, leaving the door open. He saw an older man inside with glasses and short hair who said hello to him. Anderson may have noticed that the man was about his same height—a rarity since he had to look up to most men.

Glancing around, Anderson would have seen a cluttered store with no discernible order. A stack of three steamer trunks was near the front door with a sign advertising a special price of $13.99 for the set.

Beyond that there was a row of phonographs. One of them was a Decca, its top open showing the turntable and tone arm. Looking at a glass case on one of the walls, Anderson would have counted at least twenty rifles.

(Courtesy Brown family)

What exactly was said and what happened after this

would vary but this we know: Anderson had planned on
hocking his ring, and said he didn't like the way he was
being treated by Louis Richards. Since Anderson still
owed about $60 on a conditional sales contract, Richards
told him the most he could give him was about $10 cash.

After talking with Anderson for a while, the store
manager beckoned Swienty to come into the store.

According to court records, Anderson had asked
for .30—.30 ammunition.

At this point, Richards probably turned Anderson over
to his assistant, who usually helped customers with
firearms and ammunition. Anderson, believing he had
been mistreated by Richards may have asked why
someone else had to help him and could have been told
that Swienty was a World War I veteran and knew more
about firearms than the credit manager.

Swienty went behind the glass counter and after
learning what ammunition Anderson wanted told him that
he had none of that type. Then Anderson asked about rifles
that were on display and said he wanted to see a
Remington .30—.06 with a telescopic sight attached.
Swienty opened the case, got the weapon and brought it
back and handed it to Anderson.

"How much?" Anderson asked.

"One hundred five dollars," Swienty answered.

Anderson thought a moment and then said, "That's
pretty high but, I'll take it."

* * * * *

(In 1965, under California law there was no waiting period
for people purchasing rifles or ammunition. The law was
tougher for handguns, increasing the waiting period from
three to five days in 1965.

In 2018 California had a ten-day waiting period for all firearm purchases, transfers and private sales, which must be conducted through a federal and state firearm license holder. Law enforcement people in 1965 knew if a person wanted to murder someone, a rifle was the weapon of immediate choice.)

* * * * *

Now retired San Diego and Carlsbad police officer Orville (Orv) Hale was in the vicinity at the time Anderson entered the Hub Loans & Jewelry Company.

Orv Hale
(Courtesy Orv Hale)

In an interview at his Escondido home, Hale says there was an alert system between the San Diego Police Department and downtown San Diego pawnshops if help were needed.

Orv Hale

"The alert system code name was 'Change Calls,'"
Hale said. "If a pawnshop employee was suspicious about
a customer or felt threatened, clerks were instructed to
open the cash register, pretend to look inside and then tell
the person, 'I'm almost out of change' and say they had to
call the bank. They would then dial the number for the
police and when the operator answered, the code was,
'This is Hub (or whatever shop it was) we are out of
change.' Then the police would get to the pawnshop as fast
as possible."

Although Swienty would later testify that Anderson
needed a shave, apparently his suspicions were not aroused
enough to initiate a "Change Calls" alert because this was
not mentioned in court testimony.

When Anderson asked for a box of shells, Swienty
found one and placed them on the counter next to the rifle
and with no legal restraints on the purchase, began writing
up a sales receipt for the rifle and ammunition. It was then
that Anderson reached across the counter and grabbed the
gun and shells.

"Wait a second," Swienty protested, "you can't do that."

Anderson started loading the bullets in the rifle and said,

"I want to see if the shells fit." He then backed away from the counter.

Swienty moved toward Anderson, but stopped when he heard the rifle bolt slam shut. He was staring into the barrel of the gun. Pointing the loaded rifle at Swienty from point blank range, Anderson said, "I'm going to blow your brains out, you son of a bitch."

Louis Richards, standing nearby perhaps had wondered about a moment like this and immediately said what he had likely rehearsed in his mind a thousand times. In a voice he hoped would prevent the agitated gunman from pulling the trigger he said, "If you want it, you can have it. Take it and go."

It was later determined that at the sound of Richards' voice, Anderson swung the gun away from Swienty and pointed it toward Richards. The Hub owner pleaded, "Don't shoot!" and then bolted for the front door. Immediately, there was a rifle blast.

A passer-by, Antonio Cidot heard the rifle go off and saw Richards fall to the floor, face down, arms extended, near the pawnshop's open doorway.

Antonio Cidot
(Courtesy KGTV, KFMB-TV and San Diego Police Museum)

Among those who interviewed Cidot were Chuck
Woolsey, assignment editor of KOGO-TV, pressed into
service as a reporter and Les Dobbs of KOGO-TV, doing
double duty as a news photographer and reporter.

Chuck Woolsey

Les Dobbs
(Courtesy KGTV, KFMB-TV and San Diego Police
Museum)

Eyewitness Cidot said the man (Richards) at the entrance was bleeding and his glasses were on the sidewalk. Cidot said Richards, still alive, called for police help but when Cidot saw the gunman he went to the William Penn Hotel next door and asked the clerk, C.H. Chiles, to call police.

For Ted Swienty, time must have seemed to be standing still. Terrified, Swienty bolted toward a stairway that led to the shop's second floor. Anderson glanced at Richards' lifeless body and then rushed to the open stairway where he heard Swienty racing up the steps. He fired his rifle at the clerk and knew he had not hit him when he heard Swienty yelling out a second-story window for police on the street below.

Anderson then went to Richards and knelt next to the dead man's body. His mind was racing and later he would say that his thoughts were, *God, this guy's dead.* He was scared and told himself he had to do something to protect himself. Until now, he had only been involved in minor scrapes with the law. But this was the big thing. Anderson told himself there was no way he was going to walk outside and give himself up.

Just then, Robert McLennan, a plainclothes burglary detail police officer arrived on scene and, hearing that a man inside had a gun, immediately took cover nearby.

Robert McLennan
(Courtesy San Diego Police Museum)

From his vantage point, McLennan saw another officer, William Duncan edging toward the pawnshop's front door with his handgun drawn.

William Duncan
(Courtesy San Diego Police Museum)

McLennan could see a victim lying face down in the doorway and saw Anderson inside with a rifle that had a telescopic sight and was moving toward the doorway.

McLennan watched the gunmen inside stop as Duncan

moved closer to the pawnshop's entrance. When Anderson
and Duncan confronted each other, Anderson raised his
rifle and fired at Duncan. The police officer fired back but
neither hit the other and both men retreated. Anderson then
smashed the glass pistol case open, grabbing guns and
bullets and headed toward the stairway.

Chapter 4
The Response

After Louis Richards was shot and Swienty frantically shouted for help, a police radio dispatcher sounded the alert.

Police reconstruction of radio dispatch
(Courtesy San Diego Police Museum)

The response was instantaneous and dozens of officers began arriving on the scene and started exchanging fire with Anderson. Others headed that way.

One of them was Sergeant Allen Brown. Even though he had been on duty since 3 A.M., he knew a supervisor was needed, so he went to the scene to offer his assistance.

Just in case extra firepower was required, Brown grabbed
a rifle and extra shells and ran to his police car.

Minutes later, Brown was there and saw that uniformed
officers had the building surrounded. In a nearby doorway
out of the line of fire, Brown found two detectives who
told him as much as they knew about what was going on.
A man was barricaded inside the store and had probably
killed one person and was firing at police.

(Courtesy KGTV and KFMB-TV and San Diego Police
Museum)

Two days later in *The San Diego Union,* reporter Joe
Stone quoted Brown as saying, "Three shots were fired.
They hit about 20 feet from me. They couldn't possibly
have hit me where I was standing, but they sure made it
emphatic that the man had a gun and he was not playing."

By now, the streets were echoing with the sound of
nonstop gunfire. The detectives told Brown they thought
there might be two gunmen inside the Hub. It was then
someone handed the sergeant a shotgun.

"I don't know who gave it to me," he said. "The weapons just show up at a time like that."

(Courtesy Brown family)

Among the first officers on the scene were patrolmen 33-year-old Charles David (Dave) Crow and 25-year-old Orville "Orv" Hale.

Dave Crow   Orv Hale 1961 photo
(Courtesy San Diego Police   (Courtesy Orv Hale)
Museum)

Hale was assigned to Unit 7, the police department's one-man downtown ambulance unit. The ambulance was a 1964 Ford Fairlane station wagon with a gurney behind the front seat. Crow, who passed away in February 2018, was assigned a regular downtown patrol car and it, too, was a one-man unit.

In 2018 Hale was 78, retired and living with his wife of 50 years, Caroline in Escondido, California.

Caroline and Orv Hale

He said Crow arrived ahead of him by about two minutes and was already pinned-down by the passenger side of his patrol vehicle which was positioned directly in front of the corner entrance to the pawnshop.

Dave Crow by his patrol car
(Courtesy Brown family)

In an interview at his home, Hale said, "Being aware of
gunshot sounds, I stopped my vehicle just short of the
shop's F Street windows and partially on the sidewalk.

(Courtesy KGTV, KFMB-TV and San Diego Police
Museum)

"I got out of my vehicle and took up a standing
position just clear of any gunshot activity."

* * * * *

Meantime, while officers on and off duty scrambled
from around the immediate area to reach the scene, one
call came from 16 miles to the east in El Cajon. Police
detective H.D. Earp, a distant cousin of gunfighter Wyatt
Earp said he was available, but the offer was politely
declined.

* * * * *

Gunman Robert Anderson now was out to find the
clerk who got away. Armed to the teeth, he went up the
stairway and found the second floor packed with boxes of
pawnshop junk but more importantly for him there were

more weapons: pistols, racks of rifles and ammunition. He
then entered a small, pitch-black room. The only window
was still painted over from World War II black outs.
Anderson felt his way around the room looking for the
clerk, but unknown to him, Ted Swienty was hiding face
down under a small bed, playing "possum" and hoping his
feet would not be seen sticking out. Swienty heard
someone walk by a few yards from where he lay and
closed his eyes. Surely the gunman could hear his heart
that seemed to be beating louder than a bass drum.

(Courtesy KGTV, KFMB-TV and San Diego Police
Museum)

In between occasional gunfire coming from the street
Swienty heard a high-pitched voice, which he recognized
as the gunman's.

To his relief he heard him say, "He ain't here. Son of a
bitch."

Seconds that seemed like hours passed until the

footsteps retreated. The sound of gunfire from the street continued.

* * * * *

Police were frustrated in their efforts to get into the building through a back door. One of the officers on the scene was 36-year-old detective Leigh Emmerson who exchanged gunfire with Anderson. Emmerson had to take extra precautions because he was a large target. The former basketball player at Cal Poly, San Luis Obispo stood six-feet-seven inches and drew good natured comparisons to actor Fred Gwynne, who played Officer Muldoon on the TV show "Car 54 Where are You?"

Officer Emmerson on the left, Officer Muldoon on the right.

Leigh Emmerson
(Courtesy *San Diego Union*)

Retired Captain Jim Collins, then a patrolman said, "Leigh tried to enter the shop through a back door, and the suspect fired several rounds at him. He later was able to enter with Brown (Sgt. Allen Brown)."

Jim Collins
(Courtesy San Diego Police Museum)

After Leigh Emmerson's first wife, Beverly, passed away from a heart attack in 1975 at age 45, Emmerson married Kathy Showers in 1977.

Kathy Emmerson

They remained together 29 years until his death in 2006 at age 76.

* * * * *

Another police officer who responded and tried to bring down Anderson was Lee Vaughn who was in Golden Hill in Unit 10 on his way back to headquarters when he got a radio call and headed downtown.

Lee Vaughn 1995 and 2018
(Courtesy San Diego Police Museum)

Vaughn, 80 in a 2018 telephone interview from his Seligman, Arizona home were he breeds thoroughbred horses recalled arriving at F Street near Fifth Avenue on that April morning.

"I pulled to the curb, got out of my squad car and began popping rounds," he said.

He was moved from the scene and took up a position across the street on the second floor above Pepitone's Bar. From there he caught brief glimpses of the gunman.

"He would come to the Hub's rear door a few times, open it and fire and then go back inside. With my six-inch Smith & Wesson, I took a few shots at him but never knew if I hit him."

By now, it was necessary for police to evacuate people who lived in the adjacent five-story William Penn Hotel that was over the pawnshop. After going up and down the hallways and pounding on room doors, police officers led several men with more miles on them than the 45-year-old dingy brick building in a line from the hotel east on Fifth

Avenue.

(Courtesy KGTV, KFMB-TV and San Diego Police
Museum)

   The last man in line was blind and gripped the handle
of his extended white cane while a plainclothes detective
held the tip.

(Courtesy KGTV, KFMB-TV and San Diego Police
Museum)

For others near the Hub, it was business as usual. A
mailman, following the unofficial motto of the United
States Postal Service that is inscribed on New York's
James Farley Post Office in New York City facing Penn
Station took the words to heart: "Neither snow nor rain nor
heat nor gloom of night stays these couriers from the swift
completion of their appointed rounds." The mailman was
walking down F Street delivering mail near the shootout
until two cops grabbed him and hustled him away.

A meter maid ignored the shootout. Her car was parked
directly across from the Hub on the southwest corner of
Fifth Avenue and F Street and she busily wrote tickets for
overtime parking violations.

* * * * *

More than 60 police officers now surrounded the
building and continued a barrage of fire with little idea
what they were shooting at.

(Courtesy KGTV, KFMB-TV and San Diego Police
Museum)

(Courtesy KGTV, KFMB-TV and San Diego Police Museum)

Inside, Robert Anderson, nicknamed "Rabbit" as a kid because he was small and ran fast, sprinted up and down the stairs, firing about 80 rounds out the windows to keep police at bay. As he emptied his weapons and reloaded, he was likely thinking to himself that for 28 years, no one gave him any respect, but now he was the center of attention and was fighting back at those who had put him down all his life. But deep down, despite all the excitement, as the light rain kept falling, Anderson likely knew he was fighting a losing battle. Even so, he probably kept thinking of a way to escape the building. He wasn't about to put down his weapons or give anything up.

At one point he opened the cash register by depressing large denomination keys. An investigation would show that before the murder, the last cash register transaction had been $3.00.

Anderson perhaps thought that when it got dark, with money from the cash register and a pistol, he could sneak out of the building, leave town and begin a new life.

In the pouring rain, grainy television images showed Inspector Wayne Colburn, in charge of the scene, trying

several times to call Anderson out of the building using a
bullhorn.

(Courtesy KGTV, KFMB-TV and San Diego Police
Museum)

    The gunfire from the police stopped and in the pouring
rain a voice over a bullhorn echoed in the streets. "Please
drop your weapons. Come out of the store. You see you
are surrounded. We have the necessary equipment. Now
come out!"
    Anderson answered with a barrage of bullets.

Chapter 5
The Media

Not long after the shootout began, radio stations in San Diego began telling their listeners what was happening at Fifth and F. The leading stations were KFMB AM 760 (recently switched from 540 AM), KOGO AM 600 and KSDO AM 1130. News bulletins were given and soon all stations, whatever their format were telling listeners about the firefight outside the Hub pawnshop.

Back then there were no instant live capabilities for television to broadcast directly from the scene; the mini-cam trucks with telescopic antennas, microwave connections and videotape cameras were still fifteen years away. Video for newscasts was black and white film. At the Hub shootout, couriers shuttled 100-foot cans and 400-foot magazines of .16-millimeter optical sound film from the scene to the TV stations where the film was developed in onsite labs and then cut, edited, spliced together and then put on projectors to be seen on the air. Crews talked of getting the film in the "soup" and waiting 20 minutes for it to come out of the chemicals and dry.

KFMB-TV Channel 8 and KFMB 76 AM radio were the closest to the scene with studios to the north on the corner of Fifth Avenue and Ash. KOGO-TV Channel 10 had its broadcast facilities less than five miles to the east on 47th Avenue just north of Highway 94.

The most prominent TV news figure of the day was Ray Wilson, news director and news anchor at the CBS affiliate, KFMB-TV Channel 8.

(KFMB-TV ad courtesy KFMB-TV
KOGO-TV ad courtesy KGTV)

KFMB's "The Big News" with Ray Wilson early and
Bob Regan at 11 P.M. competed fiercely against the NBC
affiliate, KOGO-TV Channel 10 with its primary news
anchors Sam Rinaker at 6 P.M. and Frank Van Cleave at
11 P.M.

(Frank Van Cleave photo courtesy KGTV and San Diego
Police Museum, KFMB-TV ad courtesy KFMB-TV)

Channel 10 first went on the air in 1953 as KFSD-TV and changed its call letters to KOGO-TV when the station was purchased by Time-Life in 1962. The current call letters of KGTV came after the station was sold to McGraw Hill in 1972.

In 1965, ABC-TV aired its programing on a Tijuana, Mexico-based station, Channel 6 XETV and offered a low-budget news broadcast. Seven months after the Hub shootout, on November 14, 1965, KAAR-TV, UHF Channel 39 signed on and began carrying ABC-TV programs. XETV Channel 6 became an independent station. But on this day, it was a news battle between Channels 8 and 10 with each station putting together extraordinary coverage of what seemed to be the story of a lifetime.

Rooftop antennas were used in 1965 since there was no cable TV. San Diego is a city with many canyons, so if you were in a good location with line of sight and high enough you could bring in Los Angeles television stations. But most people watched the local channels especially on April 8, 1965.

* * * * *

One of the first San Diego news people at the Hub shootout was 22-year-old Carl Gilman a self-confessed news "hound" and a news photographer for KFMB-TV, Channel 8.

Carl Gilman
(Courtesy KFMB-TV)

Gilman joined the station in August 1964, having dropped out of San Diego State College after a year to help support his mother and five siblings. Gilman's father had died suddenly four years earlier at the age of 42 from a heart attack.

On April 8, 1965, Gilman was scheduled to work the night shift and was not on duty when the shooting at Fifth and F began.

News photographers back then did not have company cars, similar to the one shown above to take home, but carried their equipment in their own cars for breaking stories. Today electronic and print news assignment desks have sophisticated electronic scanners that monitor police, fire and other emergency frequencies.

On that morning, Gilman had an old-fashioned tube-type radio in his car with only one frequency. That band picked up radio dispatch traffic for the San Diego police, fire department and even the dogcatcher. Gilman's radio unit took up the entire "trunk" of his Volkswagen Bug, the trunk being up front in the rear engine Beatle.

That morning as soon as Gilman heard police talking about the shootout he didn't have time to call the station and immediately began speeding toward downtown.

Interviewed in 2018, Gilman remembers, "I took Highway 94 into the city and as I got closer I could hear gunshots."

Before retiring in 2004, Gilman had a distinguished Emmy award-winning career beginning with 12 years at KFBM-TV and then 27 years freelancing that brought assignments with CBS, including segments for "60 Minutes."

Carl Gilman
(Courtesy Carl Gilman)
But what happened April 8, 1965 would be the most harrowing day of his life.

"I got there around 10:15," Gilman said, just minutes after the gun battle had begun.

"I sneaked in as close as I could and found myself pinned down and hiding next to one of two police cars in the middle of F Street that were being used as shields. Crowds of people were beginning to form on nearby corners." Gunfire was coming from inside the Hub while officers were emptying their rifles and pistols on the pawnshop. Bullets could be heard *zinging* off metal, glass, cement or wherever the shot ended up.

Gilman was carrying a small hand-held 70 DR Bell and Howell silent camera that shot black and white 16-millimeter film. The compact nature of his equipment likely enabled him not to draw attention to himself from police officers.

70 DR Bell and Howell camera
(Courtesy Carl Gilman)

The most popular sound camera of that day was the
Auricon Pro-600. They were big, bulky and the entire unit
weighed 55 pounds. The camera and film magazine were
attached to a mount that was carried on a man's shoulder
while a battery pack was draped over his other shoulder.
The sheer weight of the camera explains why women were
not TV news photographers then and why many veteran
news photographers of that time needed back operations in
later years.

Auricon Pro 600 sound camera
(Courtesy Carl Gilman)

Gilman said that someone from KFMB-TV alerted the
station that he was at the shootout scene and it was not
long until a colleague slipped past officers to reach Gilman
who handed him silver cans of the news film he had just
shot.

By this time the news people at all San Diego television stations were in full emergency mode. The newsrooms emptied out and soon photographers and reporters were at the scene but none as close as Carl Gilman. In the following photo, Gilman, wearing a tie, can be seen on the far left hunched over as officers carrying weapons and explosives rush to find a safe place to open fire.

(Courtesy Brown family)

Gilman's silent camera captured the early action but there was an urgent need to get a sound camera and soon there was one on the scene.

(Courtesy KFMB-TV, KGTV and San Diego Police
Museum)

"Del Lynam (a news photographer at KFMB-TV),"
Gilman remembers, "went to the second floor of a nearby
hotel and found a vantage point looking directly down at
the Hub. He was using a sound camera and filmed
everything."

Gilman remembers watching with fascination as police
officers kept arriving on the scene in the rain. "The cops in
their cars would drive up, get out and begin shooting.
When they emptied their guns and ran out of bullets, they
got back in their cars and drove off."

Reports were that off-duty officers, who saw the story
on television came to the scene, emptied their guns into the
building and left.

* * * * *

KFMB-TV's vice president and general manager in
1965 was George Whitney.

George Whitney
(Courtesy *Broadcasting*)

Some station employees remember Whitney as a
snobby-sort, a man who basked in the notoriety of running
a television station and used it hoping to impress those in
his social circles including his rich La Jolla friends.

For George Whitney, image was everything and he
insisted that all news employees wear coats, ties and dress
shoes while in the field, even photographers. Never mind
the story, be it fires, floods or in this case pouring rain in
the middle of a police firefight, KFMB-TV crews were to
be well-dressed.

Carl Gilman wearing his "uniform of the day" in front of
the old KFMB-TV station on Fifth and Ash.
                    (Courtesy Carl Gilman)

    Contrasting Whitney was the vice president and general
manager of KOGO-TV, Clayton Brace.

Clayton Brace
(Courtesy KGTV)

While Clayton Brace also mandated coats and ties for his newsroom personnel (the idea was from Brace's wife, Jeannine) he is remembered as a caring and cordial man who always had a smile and instilled a sense of esprit de corps at the station.

* * * * *

For Carl Gilman, trapped on the street next to a police car with bullets whizzing over his head, the on-again, off-again rain had soaked him and his jacket was getting sticky. He remained in place to the very end before returning to the station. He remembers the scenes as if they were yesterday. "It was incredible how people jumped in and performed. Secretaries normally not connected with the newsroom were running up and down the hallways, helping anywhere they could."

KFMB-TV newsroom 1970
Carl Gilman is in the middle behind the guy with glasses
looking to his left.

A chalkboard in the newsroom was continually
changed as news director Ray Wilson, editor Stu Batt and
the evening news producers decided how the newscasts
would be structured.

Stu Batt
(Courtesy Carl Gilman)

Gilman was told to get a sound camera and go with the late Harold Keen, still considered the Dean of San Diego TV news reporters.

Harold Keen
(Courtesy KFMB-TV)

They would do interviews in the pressroom at police headquarters at Pacific Highway and Market Street.

* * * * *

There were other news people not as fortunate as Gilman to get close to the scene. One was longtime radio newsman Reid Carroll. Then 31 years old and working for the Mexican-owned station XTRA, Carroll headed for downtown hoping to capture sounds of the shooting on his tape recorder.

Reid Carroll
(Courtesy Reid Carroll)

In a 2018 interview, Carroll, then 84 remembered, "I got there at 11 A.M. and was almost arrested for trying to get close. We had no cell phones back then to call in a report, so I left at 1 P.M. and went back to the studio and used wire reports the rest of the day."

* * * * *

The *San Diego Union* gave its readers the story the next morning. The headline read **Downtown S.D. Gun Battle Rages 4 Hours; One Slain.** Below that was Dope User Holes Up In Pawnshop; Wounded, Seized.

Reporter Dick Bowman characterized Anderson as "A berserk laborer."

An hour into the shootout and standoff, no one knew if pawnshop manager Louis Richards was still alive and Sergeant Allen Brown volunteered to try and get to him. To keep the gunman pinned down, Detective Sergeant Carl O. Davis fired three tear gas shells into the shop.

Carl Davis
(Courtesy San Diego Police Museum)

"Everyone was well placed," Brown later told reporters. He and Patrolman Robert Augustine put on gas masks but then the rain intensified. "The goggles on the mask fogged up and we could not see," Brown said.

Bob Augustine
(Courtesy San Diego Police Museum

They discarded the gas masks and fell back to let some
of the tear gas drift away. It was then that spectators on F
Street could be heard letting out a collective gasp as
Brown crept toward the pawnshop's front door while
Augustine provided cover to his right.

(Courtesy KGTV, KFMB-TV and San Diego Police
Museum)

"I didn't know if he was dead or not," Brown said later,
"I only knew I had to try and drag him to safety."

(Courtesy Brown family)

The sergeant then put on a helmet and cumbersome metal bulletproof vest and while officers on both sides of the pawnshop fired away to give Brown and Augustine cover, the sergeant reached Richards.

(Courtesy KGTV, KFMB-TV and San Diego Police Museum)

(Courtesy KGTV, KFMB-TV and San Diego Police Museum)

Moments later Sergeant Brown turned from the doorway and after flashing thumbs-down, signaled that Richards was dead.

It was then that other police officers, including patrolman Orv Hale used a rolling gurney from the police ambulance to reach the pawnshop manager's body.

(Courtesy KGTV, KFMB-TV and San Diego Police Museum)

TV news film and a photograph by Bob Redding of the *San Diego Union* showed three crouching police officers on the sidewalk under a window.

(Courtesy *San Diego Union* and San Diego Police Museum)

The officer to the left is Orv Hale pushing the police gurney that had been lowered to a few inches off the sidewalk. On the gurney is an unidentified uniformed police motorcycle officer with his hands on the sidewalk while an unidentified plainclothes detective is near the store entrance.

More gunfire from police kept the suspect pinned down and quickly officers, including Sergeant Brown (closest to the post) lifted Richards' lifeless body on the gurney.

(Courtesy KGTV, KFMB-TV and San Diego Police
Museum)

After securing Richards' body, Hale (left wearing a
helmet) and the motorcycle officer scooted sideways along
the sidewalk on F Street, rolling and pulling the gurney.

(Courtesy KGTV, KFMB-TV and San Diego Police
Museum)

Following this, they placed the gurney with Richards'
body in the police ambulance. Orv Hale eventually took
the body to the county morgue.

(Courtesy KGTV, KFMB-TV and San Diego Police
Museum)

Elsewhere, reporters on the scene crouched in the doorway of the Hi–Life Bar on F Street to cover the action. Others such as KFMB-TV news photographer Carl Gilman who managed to get next to police cars in the middle of the street were stuck in place as rain continued to fall and bullets were exchanged back and forth.

* * * * *

Robert Crandall, the 52-year-old editor for the San Diego *Independent* ran as close as he could to the action. He is shown in the following photos crouching in front of Gilman and behind another man.

(Courtesy Brown family)

(Courtesy KGTV, KFMB-TV and San Diego Police Museum)

Crandall remained there for a while and then in the photos that follow he is shown moving toward the sidewalk near the William Penn Hotel's entrance.

(Courtesy KGTV, KFMB-TV and San Diego Police Museum)

(Courtesy KGTV, KFMB-TV and San Diego Police Museum)

Crandall would never file a report or tell what
happened because minutes later, although not shown on
film, Crandall suddenly crumpled and fell to the ground.
Had he been hit by a bullet? Coming to his side and
risking being hit by gunfire were *San Diego Union*
photographer Bob Redding and San Diego police officer
Ed Perkins.

They had to get him to safety and draped Crandall over
Redding's shoulders and took the newspaperman to a
doorway of a nearby jewelry store on F Street.

(Courtesy KFMB-TV and San Diego Police Museum)

Ed Perkins
(Courtesy Ed Perkins)
Efforts of Redding, Perkins and Perkins' partner,
officer William Pfahler, to revive Crandall with artificial
respiration were futile. After being taken to a nearby
hospital by police ambulance, it was determined Crandall
had suffered a heart attack and was pronounced dead.

* * * * *

In 2018, Ed Perkins, 85, lived with his wife, Arline in
Yuma, Arizona.

Arline and Ed Perkins
(Courtesy Ed Perkins)

In telephone interviews, Perkins said that he and his partner Bill Pfahler were working the Vice detail that day in the Gaslamp Quarter and shortly after the shooting began saw Robert Crandall fall to the sidewalk. They thought he had been shot. Nearby was *Union* newspaper photographer Redding. The two of them rushed to Crandall's side and carried him away.

"We pumped his chest," Perkins remembers. "But abandoned it when it was obvious it was a lost cause."

* * * * *

Ed Perkins first pinned on a badge for the SDPD in 1957.

Twenty-four years later, in 1981, he was injured and forced to leave the department by the City. With a letter of recommendation from then police chief Bill Kolender; Perkins got a job in Colorado as a chief deputy where he finished out his career.

Perkins son, Curtis was a motorcycle officer and retired from the San Diego Police Department in 2015 after twenty years service.

* * * * *

In 2018, Bill Pfalhler, 80, lived with his wife, Linda in Sun City West, Arizona.

William Pfahler 1959
(Courtesy William Pfahler)

William and Linda Pfahler
(Courtesy William Pfahler)

In a telephone interview, Pfahler said when he and his partner learned about the shooting at the Hub, once they drove up to the scene and heard all the shooting, "It was obvious that with just two snub-nose revolvers between us, we couldn't get in there to say hello to him (the gunman)."

Pfahler kept out of the line of fire and remembers hearing the machine gun bursts triggered by Sergeant Sam Chasteen.

(Note: After being promoted to Sergeant, William W. Pfahler in 1988 was awarded the police department's Lifesaving Medal for his role in supervising negotiations with a despondent man who was threatening to jump from the San Diego-Coronado Bay Bridge. On January 4, 1988,

Sergeant Pfahler went to the scene and found the man
standing on a narrow steel beam outside the bridge's
railing. After more than two hours, Pfahler saw that the
man was preparing to jump. The citation reads:
"Disregarding your personal safety, you grabbed the
subject's arm and barred it against the bridge railing as he
kicked free in an unsuccessful attempt to jump from the
bridge.
"Your quick action in the face of extreme danger saved the
life of a fellow human being. You are commended for your
courage and your commitment to the citizens of our City."

   The citation was signed by Pfahler's commanding
officer, Commander Larry K. Gore and Chief of Police,
William B. Kolender.)

William Pfahler and Chief Kolender 1988
(Courtesy William Pfahler)

* * * * *

During the Hub shootout, reporters and photographers were allowed incredible access to the crime scene. The gun battle had been going on for an hour before police roped off access to the streets and sidewalks a block away at every intersection. Video shows news media people crouched behind police cars in the middle of the street and positioned next to officers firing rifles and a machine gun.

When the shooting broke out in one of downtown's busiest districts, some people were still arriving for work. And while a line of police cars finally cordoned off intersections, crowds of rubberneckers were standing a block from the battle, well within range of gunfire or ricocheted shots. Police tried their best to keep the curious out of harm's way. Some people flattened themselves against buildings and storefronts. Columnist Lew Scarr, writing the next day on April 9 observed, "Whenever there was a shot, almost everyone ducked instinctively. 'Look at 'em pull in their heads,' a man in a flannel shirt with a wrinkled collar said. 'If you can hear the shot it ain't goin' do you any good to duck,' he said."

Scarr wrote, "Suddenly there was a hollow boom. 'Tear gas,' a man in a Navy chief's uniform said knowingly. There was another hollow boom and smoke billowed briefly in the street."

(Courtesy KGTV, KFMB-TV and San Diego Police
Museum)

Scarr observed, "The wind on F Street was blowing
from the east. In 35 seconds the cloud of tear gas had
reached the crowd at Fourth and F. The crowd wept openly
for 10 minutes after the sweet smell of gas had been
dissipated."

"How can he stand that?" someone asked. "He's got
that stuff right in there with him and it doesn't bother him.
Here I am out here in the open and it makes me sick."

Scarr wrote that the sound of a small caliber pistol was
heard. "He's using a pop gun," someone said with a sneer
in his voice.

The man with the wrinkled collar was disgusted. "That
little old pop gun can make an awful big hole in your head,"
he said.

Hours passed with the rain standing six inches in some
places. Scarr said people walked through it seemingly
without noticing it.

* * * * *

Ken O'Brien, who rose to the rank of Deputy Police

Chief in his 31-year-career had been on the force ten years
when the Hub shootout happened. He remembered with
disdain how the crowds reacted to the incident.

(Courtesy San Diego Police Museum)

"It was demeaning," O'Brien, said in an October 24,
1965 interview with the *San Diego Reader* "that the
crowds were cheering for the villain. And the press was a
pain in the ass, too. Everyone was much closer than they
should have been.

(Courtesy KGTV, KFMB-TV and San Diego Police
Museum)

"But then, it was one of the most significant events we'd experienced in the city, and it happened at the worst place, at the worst time."

* * * * *

Frank Rhodes was a newspaper columnist for the *San Diego Union* and on Sunday, April 11 wrote about "ECHOES FROM 5th & F: Executives of Land Title received a running account of Friday's (it actually was Thursday's) four-hour gunfight by phone. Fred Woods, the Borrego Springs real estate man, was walking to the Land Title Building when he came within range of fire. A policeman shouted him into a bar with orders to stay there until told to come out. With each development outside, Woods phoned L.T.'s legal department, reporting it to Ray Kelly who related the news. Woods had to do something during the long wait. He has been on the wagon two years."

Also in his column after mentioning Robert Crandall, the editor of the *San Diego Independent* who died of a heart attack at the shooting scene, Rhodes wrote: "While in his car, William Lange was shocked to find himself confronted by a man with a gun. He feared it was a holdup until the man ordered him to lie on the floor of the car and ran to another auto. Lange complied but it was hard to do. He drives a little sport car."

* * * * *

Personal stories of what people were doing at the time of the Hub shooting continued for months. In August 1965 from Central News Column was this:

"During the big acclaimed shoot out at the loan company, Dave Crow, being long on bravery and short on time to think of a way out of it, got himself a command position for being one of the first on the scene. He found himself kneeling behind the fender of a car, right in the

line of fire and he stayed there for the duration. A couple
of weeks later he was in a service station where a friend
asked him about his part in the shooting and Dave told him
that he was the one, in the now famous photo, who was
kneeling next to the car.

(Courtesy Brown family)

A girl overheard that and said that she had been part of
the crowd and noticed Dave in action. Then she said, "You
must be Catholic, no one else could kneel down that long."

* * * * *

In 1965, after seven years on the job, a 32-year-old
divorcee from Indiana was on her way to becoming the
best-known police radio dispatch operator in the history of
the San Diego Police Department. Billie Wegener would
work as a dispatch operator for an incredible 45 years.

(Courtesy S.D.P.O.A.)

Billie Crow
(Courtesy San Diego Police Museum)

In a July 2018 telephone interview, at age 85 Billie
sounded vibrant and happily talked about the past. She
said she was not on duty the morning of the Hub Loans
shootout because nearly all of her time as a dispatcher was
spent working preferred evening and swing shifts. She
laughed and said she probably was still in bed when the

shootout began.

She did, however, verify what retired police officer Orv Hale said about a secret code that existed with shop clerks downtown in which they could call a police number and say "change," which was the code word for someone possibly dangerous being there. When the code word was used, the responding police would not know what to expect since it could be a violent person. So a neutral term was used to avoid making the person suspicious.

* * * * *

One of the many officers who heard Billie Crow's voice over the radio on a daily basis was patrolman Dave Crow who had been on the force for nine years and was among the first officers to arrive at the Hub. He liked how she sounded but did not meet her until 1966, a year after the shootout.

The two dated for six years until 1972 when Dave got a "10-4" after asking Billie to marry him.

Dave and Billie Crow
(Courtesy San Diego Police Museum)

Dave and Billie Crow
(Courtesy San Diego Police Museum)

The couple was married 46 years before Dave Crow passed away February 25, 2018.

Their granddaughter, Amanda Thomas in 2018 said, "I was told several times as a child that many people found my grandma's voice rather soothing but that was probably because she was calm during very intense moments and that alone is comforting.

"Her uncanny ability to help guide police to their desired location, while keeping a cool head, using backstreets and alternate routes (during a time before Google Maps or even MapQuest) was immeasurably helpful to the 'boots on the ground.' For someone born in Indiana, she definitely passes as more of a San Diego native than many people I grew up with."

Amanda says Dave and Billie each had a previous marriage end in divorce. She says the running joke at the time was that Billie would not marry Dave until he made lieutenant. "I think they both knew they were going to get married but wanted to take it slow."

* * * * *

After they were married, Billie Crow said she and her husband didn't talk much about what happened at the Hub shootout. And that extended to other conversations. Her granddaughter said they rarely spoke about their professional lives with their family. To them, Amanda says, "It was just work."

Dave and Billie Crow were modest about their professional talents and accomplishments and knew all too well the dangers police officers face every day they put on their uniform or the instant life or death decisions Billie had to make as a dispatcher. So when it came to the Hub shootout, there was no need to drudge up any what-might-have-been. Stating the obvious, "I just was glad he was alive," she said. They preferred to keep things light, as seen in a photo of Dave at a fund-raising event.

(Courtesy Crow family)

Amanda said that her grandfather told her that it was her grandmother who helped him be a better man/father/grandfather. He said he used to be a bit hot headed, but that her grandmother "mellowed him down."

And truth be known, Billie Crow told her granddaughter

that she dated before Dave Crow came into her life, but kept quiet about it out of respect for him. Amanda speculates on the reasons her grandmother chose her grandfather who was "head-over-heels about her even though he was not very expressive." She thinks it was a combination of factors. They had a lot in common with police work and past relationships and they shared similar political and religious ideology. Amanda also thinks her grandmother wanted to be a step-mom to Dave's two children and wanted someone who was not all talk. Says Amanda, "My G'pa definitely wasn't much of a talker, well not compared to my G'ma who had the gift of gab."

(Courtesy Crow family)

(Courtesy Brown family)

As for Dave Crow and his ability to kneel for a long time, what about when he popped the marriage question to Billie? Amanda asked her grandmother that and said, "She was pretty sure he proposed on at least one knee."

Chapter 6
The Assault

Officers, including Dave Crow, Orv Hale and Allen Brown who responded to the Hub shootout scene quickly realized they needed more protection from the gunman than crouching behind their squad cars.

(Courtesy KGTV, KFMB-TV and San Diego Police Museum)

The initial strategy was to get as close to the building as possible to try and force the suspect out by using tear gas. The first cover barrier was a Coca Cola delivery truck that was heading north on Fifth Avenue.

Whatever deliveries George Parks of east San Diego had planned that morning with his Coke truck; his route was interrupted before he reached F Street.

Craig Colburn, then 26 and the son of Inspector Wayne Colburn, the officer in charge of the scene, was a supervisor that day for the Coca Cola Bottling Company in San Diego and the downtown area was part of his territory.

Craig and Wayne Colburn
(Courtesy Craig Colburn)

In a 2018 interview, Colburn remembers driver George Parks returning to the company that afternoon and telling him what happened.

"The first thing he said was something about what an incredible day he just had. He told me while driving downtown he saw a police officer in front of his truck come to a sudden stop. The officer got out, ran up to the truck and with one hand raised for Parks to stop and with the other hand he began firing his pistol at the second floor of the Hub building."

At the time of the shootout, even if he wanted to go to the scene, Colburn said he could not have gotten close because access was blocked.

(Courtesy KGTV, KFMB-TV and San Diego Police Museum)

Driver George Parks later told reporters, "I stopped and jumped out. I ran across the street and a minute later a policeman jumped into my truck and moved it ahead a few feet."

(Courtesy Brown family)

The truck was parked along Fifth Street facing west and
provided a shield along the Hub's south side at the
intersection of Fifth and F. Craig Colburn says the truck
was an older model with no top over the bottles and had a
steel plate on the side that served to protect the officers
standing next to it.

(Courtesy Brown family)

Officers wanted to use tear gas in the store but to have access they needed to break the large thick front windows that sided the Hub. The July 1965 issue of *True Detective* reported that Sergeant Brown went to Inspector Wayne Colburn, the officer in charge and made a suggestion:

"Inspector, I think Augustine (Patrolman Robert Augustine) and I can reach that pop bottle truck parked in front of the store," Brown said. "We can use the bottles to break the windows—make it easier for us to shoot in the tear gas."

"Okay, go to it," said Inspector Colburn.

Sergeant Brown and Augustine ran for a short distance and then dropped to the pavement. To stay out of the gunman's line of fire, they crawled on their stomachs the last several yards to reach the Coke truck.

News footage showed the officers flinging quart-sized Coke bottles over the truck and into the glass.

(Courtesy KGTV, KFMB-TV and San Diego Police Museum)

Sometimes a bottle would reach the building but not the window, breaking close to the sidewalk. A 1990 *Los Angeles Times* newspaper story by Richard Serrano quoted key shop operator Armond Viora who worked across the street and was joined by hundreds of other bystanders. Viora said, "When the Coke bottles missed, the crowd actually booed."

Truck driver Parks kept track of how many bottles officers used and later submitted a damage report to his employer, the Coca Cola Bottling Company. He said officers shattered three 26-ounce bottles and one six pack of Coca Cola and eight bottles of Tab to break windows. The City of San Diego later said it would not pay for any of the broken bottles or damage to the Coke truck from ricocheted bullets or the Hub pawnshop's destruction.

Police also used a Lucky Lager beer truck driven by
Ben Calvert of Spring Valley. The truck was dented in a
few places where bullets ricocheted but Calvert said no
beer bottles were broken. The city refused to pay for
damage to the truck.

(Courtesy KGTV and San Diego Police Museum)

Police officers were able to fire several tear gas shells
into the store but high winds blew most of the fumes back
into the faces of officers and a growing number of
onlookers who were standing about 75 feet from the store.

* * * * *

Word-of-mouth advice was quickly passed, "Don't
wipe your eyes. Let tears wash the gas away."

The smell of gun smoke and tear gas was everywhere.
At intervals a police whistle blew and officers shifted
positions and that was followed by heavy gunfire.

A sergeant on the scene told reporters, "I think the
(expletive) is hiding behind a counter in there. He must
have eyes made of stone to take that gas."

(Courtesy KGTV, KFMB-TV and San Diego Police
Museum)

Orv Hale, the driver of the police ambulance that was
parked near the Hub and one of those who risked his life to
remove the body of Louis Richards from the scene, offered
an explanation how Anderson was not overcome by the
tear gas.

Interviewed 53 years after the shootout Hale said,
"There were large signs above the first floor in front of
windows on the second floor. Anderson could stick his
head out the window every now and then to breathe fresh
air and not be seen by the officers on the street."

Hub Loans neon signs that covered some windows

(Courtesy KGTV, KFMB-TV and San Diego Police
Museum)

The building without the signs

The *San Diego Union* quoted a policeman in a yellow rain slicker who said, "He's got all the guns in the world in that pawnshop and the place is probably loaded with ammunition." A rifle bullet fired by the gunman then smashed a large hole in the window of the nearby San Diego Key Shop on F Street.

Spectators a block away in each direction surged against police lines and had mixed reactions to what was unfolding in front of them.

San Diego Union reporter Kay Jarvis wrote that some cheered for the gunman inside while others spoke out loudly begging for someone "to talk some sense into him."

They stepped off curbs to stand in the gutter as police shouted, "Get back, for God's sake, what are you people trying to do?"

Onlookers gawked at the drama, seemingly feasting on the violent confrontation. When hunger of a different kind was felt, people retreated into nearby pizza parlors or delis and emerged with slices of pizza or hero sandwiches. Reporter Jarvis saw an elderly man struggle to pull a wine bottle from the pocket of his dirt-stained jacket. He said to no one in particular, "I wish the cops would let me in there—I'd have that guy out of there in a second."

A street companion replied, "Oh, relax and enjoy the show. It's better than television."

Nearby it was business as usual at card rooms. Men huddled under overhead lights in smoke-filled rooms. Their only interest in the shootout was to take bets on the final count of casualties.

* * * * *

About two hours into the shootout and standoff, police needed a better and safer way to get closer to the building. So, shortly before noon, police decided to borrow an armored car from Loomis. The 50,000-pound vehicle normally used for cash handling was pressed into service to deal with the lone gunman, an irony since Loomis originally was part of Wells Fargo, a company with links to the stagecoaches of the Old West that were the targets of gunmen.

(Courtesy KFMB-TV)

(Courtesy KGTV, KFMB-TV and San Diego Police Museum)

At first, the gray, bulletproof car was backed from the intersection over the curb near the store's entrance. The idea was to allow officers to fire straight inside from a gun port. Several blasts were fired but a cement post in front limited the target area.

So it was decided a better position was to position the armored car on the sidewalk facing west along the F Street side of the Hub so its gun ports could give officers more openings to shoot into the pawnshop.

Soon, an officer in the armored car with a machine gun fired a terrific volley of shots. The bullets shredded guitars hanging from the ceiling and ripped to shreds coats and vests on a rack, riddling nearly every item in the store from television sets to record players.

At precisely 12:02 a sustained blast of a Thompson machine gun fired by Sergeant Sam Chasteen on the street took out almost the entire west window. Chasteen had become familiar with machine guns having used them in the Army when he was in counter intelligence.

Sergeant Brown and three other officers inside the
armored car now raked the inside of the shop with fire
from another machine gun and three shotguns while
Sergeant Chasteen continued with Tommy gun bursts from
the Fifth Avenue and F Street side of the scene.

Sgt. Sam Chasteen
(Courtesy KGTV, KFMB-TV and San Diego Police
Museum)

After what was blown apart crashed on the pawnshop's
tile floor with thuds and tinkling glass there was silence.
Had one of the bullets found its mark? Was the lone
gunman wounded or dead? The answer was two-fold; a
sharp crack of rifle fire from the store and lighter pops
from a pistol. The gunman was still alive and seemed to

switch weapons continuously as he ran up and down the stairs in the store's rear; something that had caused the first officers on the scene to think more than one gunman was inside. He was firing rifles, revolvers and pistols. For a few minutes he used a high-powered .30 caliber rifle, then he switched to a .22 caliber pistol, then to a .38 revolver, shooting wildly.

At 12:25 P.M. Patrol Captain Howard Charman, with a high-powered rifle and a telescope site in his hands joined Inspector Colburn.

Howard Charman
(Courtesy San Diego Police Museum)

He said was going to take up a position in the second story of the Sommers Building across the street from the Hub.

Charman found his vantage point and being a rifle sharpshooter told the men around him, "Maybe I can hit him from here."

He aimed and fired several times. Shaking his head he said, "I've gotten off a couple of shots, but I don't know if I hit the guy. He's a constant moving target and hard to see. When he fires all you can see is his forearm."

All the while, straddling the curb behind the armored car was the police ambulance with the body of Hub manager Louis Richards inside.

(Courtesy KGTV, KFMB-TV and San Diego Police Museum)

A story shared with the author is that shortly after the Hub shootout began, a San Diego patrol officer had just booked a suspect at the central jail when the watch commander yelled at him to move his cruiser over to the armory and haul ammunition to the scene. Once there, with the sound of gunfire and in the pouring rain the officer began loading clips for Sam Chasteen's machine gun. He and Chasteen were crouched down next to a brick wall along Fifth Avenue south of the Hub entrance. Suddenly, Chasteen staggered from a bleeding wound on his forehead.

At 12:50 PM, a shout echoed on the street. "An officer's been hit—get an ambulance!" Sergeant Chasteen had fallen to the sidewalk and blood was oozing from a head wound. No one could tell if he had been hit directly or by a ricocheted shot.

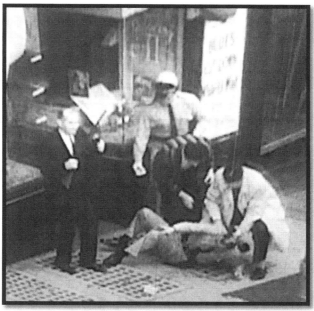

(Courtesy KGTV, KFMB-TV and the San Diego Police Museum)

The officer, who had been giving Chasteen ammunition, ripped a piece of cloth from his uniform sleeve for a bandage.

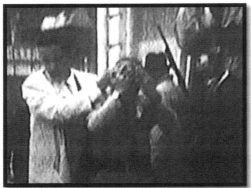

(Courtesy KGTV, KFMB-TV and San Diego Police
Museum)

With the body of Louis Richards in a nearby ambulance,
there was no time to wait for another ambulance so with
Chasteen holding the make-shift bandage to his head,
fellow officers helped him to a squad car.

(Courtesy KGTV, KFMB-TV and San Diego Police
Museum)

(Courtesy KGTV, KFMB-TV and San Diego Police
Museum)

It turned out that Chasteen had been injured after a shot
was fired his way from the pawnshop. He ducked and
bashed his forehead on a bolt that was protruding from a

steel bar. Chasteen was loaded in the car and whisked away in yet another twist to the tangled standoff. Moments later, another officer picked up Chasteen's machine gun and immediately the gun's *rat-tat-tat* was heard with bullets flying into the Hub.

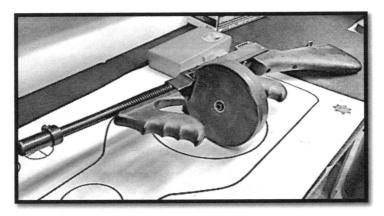

Chasteen's 1928 machine gun is now part of the San Diego Police Department's firing range memorabilia.

In 2018, Sam Chasteen, 86, lived with his caregiver wife, Sharon in San Diego. The one-time tough Sergeant was struggling with physical challenges and was deaf, blind in one eye with Glaucoma and afflicted with Alzheimer's.

Sam Chasteen
(Courtesy Sharon Chasteen)

At 1:05 PM, three hours after Louis Richards was murdered, the day's heaviest rain came in sheets. Sweeping in from Mexico, the rain soaked police, media and hundreds of spectators. It was nearly impossible to find shelter and as the gunman and police kept shooting, some drenched looky-loos returned to their offices or went home.

(Courtesy KGTV, KFMB and San Diego Police Museum)

At 1:20 PM, Sergeant Brown and other officers in the armored car used a long pole to clear a shelf in the front of the pawnshop. Everything on the shelves clattered to the floor giving police a better line of fire from across F Street. Once that was done, bullets riddled the store.

(Courtesy KGTV, KFMB-TV and San Diego Police
Museum)

The armored car was moved back slightly for a better
vantage point and a TV news reporter while the camera
was rolling talked over a microphone as if he were
broadcasting live from the scene.

"One of the officers said he (the suspect) may be in the
far rear corner. They're moving back to get a better
vantage point."

A close-up showed a shotgun poking out the gun port.

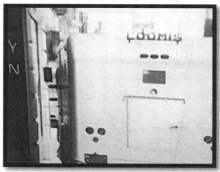

(Courtesy KGTV, KFMB-TV and San Diego Police
Museum)

The reporter continued. "While all this firing is going on, inside the police ambulance right behind the armored car, the body of the credit manager of the outfit, killed when this fighting began."

(Courtesy KGTV, KFMB-TV and San Diego Police Museum)

While the armored car was bulletproof, it was not tear gas proof. At one point after firing more tear gas canisters into the store there was a shift in the wind and it blew the tear gas out the broken windows. The fumes enveloped the armored car and got inside through the gun portals. Five officers inside the truck were eventually forced out.

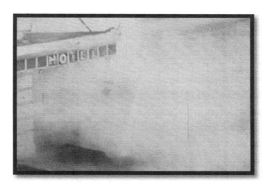

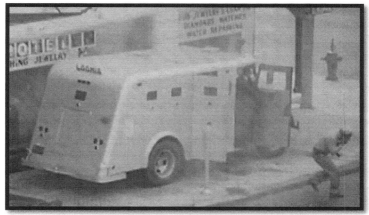

(Courtesy KGTV, KFMB-TV and San Diego Police Museum)

(Courtesy KGTV, KFMB-TV and San Diego Police
Museum)

Sergeant Bob Augustine recovers from the tear gas
(Courtesy Brown family)

Word was then passed that police might bring in someone from the Navy with hand grenades. For Sergeant Allen Brown, that rekindled memories of his service as an Army paratrooper lieutenant in World War II when he used concussion grenades to clear caves during combat on Okinawa.

Another warning to the gunman was heard over the police bull horn, "Put down your weapon and come out with your hands over your head. If you don't, we are going to fire concussion grenades." The threat was repeated and was answered with more gunfire from Anderson.

* * * * *

At 1:34 PM, 32-year-old Frank Morales a Navy Gunner's Mate Third Class showed up.

(Courtesy KGTV, KFMB-TV and San Diego Police Museum)

(Courtesy KGTV, KFMB-TV and San Diego Police
Museum)

Reporter Robert Zimmerman, writing in the *San Diego
Union* the next day said that Morales, from the destroyer
escort Bauer (DE-1025) and on shore patrol duty was
driving north toward San Diego on Highway 101 past
National City. He heard on the police radio in his Shore
Patrol truck that the police were looking for a gunner's
mate who was familiar with concussion grenades.

Morales, a 14-year Navy veteran, volunteered by radio
to help out and he was told to drive directly to Fifth and F
and report to the police.

Zimmerman wrote that a police car was sent to the
Naval Station to pick up six concussion grenades from the
tank landing ship Tioga County (LST-1048), which had
some of the weapons on board. The reporter then
explained that concussion grenades are used to simulate
torpedo hits and depth charges in submarine warfare
exercises. A Navy spokesman said the grenades produce

more of a shock wave than a blast effect and, if detonated
in a room, would be more likely to knock down and stun a
man than kill him.

Morales met with the officer in charge of the scene,
Inspector Wayne Colburn.

(Courtesy KGTV, KFMB-TV and San Diego Police
Museum)

At first, Morales said, the plan was for him to instruct
police officers in how to use the grenades. Then they
decided it would be safer for Morales to toss the first one
in and he agreed.

(Courtesy KGTV, KFMB-TV and San Diego Police Museum)

Shielded and holding two grenades, Morales waits to go into action.
(Courtesy KGTV, KFMB-TV and San Diego Police Museum)

"I put on a helmet and the bulletproof vest while we were still behind that truck in the street, and then they covered me while I ran up to the store and got behind the concrete post in front of the door," Morales said.

  With police providing a hail of covering fire, the three
photos that follow show Morales at the post, winding up
and like a right-handed baseball pitcher throwing the
grenade.
  Zimmerman quoted Morales as saying later, "I waited
one second after I pulled the pin. The manufacturer says
the grenade will go off in three to five seconds. I figured
by waiting one second, there wouldn't be time for the guy
inside to pick it up and throw it back out."

(Courtesy KGTV, KFMB-TV and San Diego Police
Museum)

(Courtesy KGTV, KFMB-TV and San Diego Police
Museum)

Once the grenade was thrown in the building, horrified police officers and media, some not knowing Morales' understanding of concussion grenades saw the Navy man linger at the post.

In the background frantic police shouted in unison, "Take off! Take off!"

Two seconds later, Morales turned and ran. You can see him in the photo just before the grenade went off in a bright orange ball of fire that shattered the front windows, filling the shop with smoke.

(Courtesy KGTV, KFMB-TV and San Diego Police Museum)

It was then that police warily approached the front entrance.

(Courtesy KGTV, KFMB-TV and San Diego Police
Museum)

Chapter 7
The Capture

As soon as the grenade went off, Morales followed a group of police officers into the pawnshop. To their surprise the gunman had run up a staircase to the second-story loft and very much alive, was shooting back at them.

Morales said that Inspector Colburn asked him if he were ready to toss another grenade and the gunner's mate replied that he was as ready as he'd ever be.

"Then I ran up about seven of the steps and threw the second one," he said. "I think that one really shook him up."

The blast blew out a wall and the mezzanine of an adjoining tailor shop on Fifth Avenue. Debris shot into the street hitting parked cars.

Making his flight to safety, Morales said he decided to head for what he thought was the door to the street. Instead he ran into what turned out to be the door to the pawnshop's safe.

"There was already a policeman in there," Morales said, "and he told me, 'Hey, there's no more room in here.'"

Soon Morales was out of the store and behind the Coke truck, getting a third grenade ready as more officers crouched in front of the entrance.

(Courtesy KGTV, KFMB-TV and San Diego Police
Museum)

By now scores of spectators were nearby wondering
what would happen next.

(Courtesy KGTV, KFMB-TV and San Diego Police
Museum)

Led by Sergeant Brown, several policemen charged into the pawnshop. He describes in detail his confrontation with the gunman in the next chapter.

* * * * *

Thinking the danger had ended, the crowd surged past police barricades.

"Get back!" an officer yelled. "We haven't got him yet."

That forced some of the spectators to retreat, who then ducked into doorways or crouched behind parked cars.

Several more gunshots were heard along with shouting from inside the pawnshop. At that point spectators rushed toward the wrecked store only to be held back by rain-soaked policemen carrying shotguns, machine guns and rifles.

Inside the store, smoke lingered from small fires started when concussion grenades were tossed into the pawnshop. Officers walked on broken glass while a stretcher was carried in through the front entrance. Spectators outside wondered if it was for the gunman or had a police officer been hit?

Officers carried the stretcher up the steps to the mezzanine, followed by a man in a suit and tie. Referred to by officers as "Doc," he was Dr. Robert Williams who served as the San Diego Police Department's physician. Dr. Williams quickly reached the second floor and saw the gunman, Robert Anderson. He had a black glove on his left hand and was lying in a pool of blood, the result of the final confrontation between the suspect and Sergeant Brown. Later it would be learned that minutes earlier Sergeant Brown had crept up a dark stairway to a loft with other officers behind him.

When he reached the top, he heard two clicks from
a .38-caliber pistol.

Sergeant Brown would say, "He (Anderson) had put
incorrect ammunition in the gun, ammunition he had found
in the store. Sometimes it fired, sometimes it didn't."
Brown then shot Anderson three times with his shotgun
from four feet away.

When Dr. Williams got to the wounded man he found
Sergeant Brown, still seething over Anderson trying to kill
him, holding the suspect down with his foot to his throat.
The doctor quickly applied tourniquets to both of
Anderson's arms. A blanket was draped over the gunman
and officers strapped him to the stretcher and carried him
downstairs.

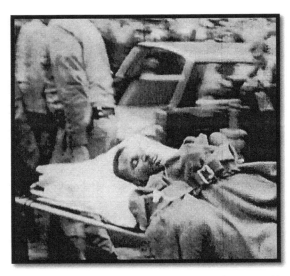

(Courtesy KGTV, KFMB-TV and San Diego Police
Museum)

Sergeant Brown then slowly came down the steps from the mezzanine and told reporters what he had done.

"I had to shoot him or be shot," he said in no uncertain terms. "I hit him in the arm and abdomen. When you get right down to it, there was nobody between me and Anderson. I wouldn't ask anybody to do what I did . . . but it seemed it was just something that had to be done at the time."

Days later a senior police official summed up the final moments by saying, "He simply had more guts than anyone else there."

The wounded man squirmed in pain under straps that held him to the stretcher. Reporters said his eyes rolled with pain and his mouth was slightly open.

As Anderson was carried out, people on the street got their first glimpse of the suspect and were likely surprised at how small he was. The four-hour standoff in which police had thrown everything at Anderson except the proverbial kitchen sink suggested the suspect was larger than life. In reality, at 5-5 and barely a hundred pounds, he didn't take up much room on the stretcher that was easily handled by officers on four sides.

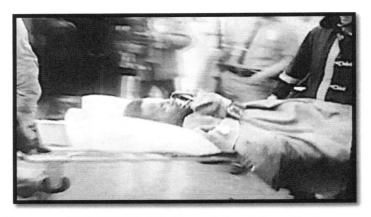

(Courtesy KGTV, KFMB-TV and San Diego Police
Museum)

(Courtesy KGTV, KFMB-TV and San Diego Police
Museum)

As Anderson was put in the ambulance, his eyes were
open and he was aware of people around him.

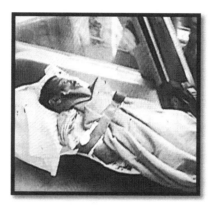

(Courtesy KGTV, KFMB-TV and San Diego Police Museum)

When a TV news photographer put his camera close to the ambulance window Anderson turned his head to the left. Above the roof of the car in the middle of the photo, one can see the top of Frank Morales's head, the gunner's mate who threw the two hand grenades.

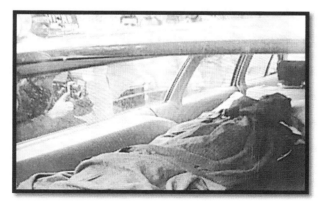

(Courtesy KGTV, KFMB-TV and San Diego Police Museum)

Minutes later, with Anderson inside, the ambulance left and headed to the County Hospital five minutes north in Hillcrest.

(Courtesy KGTV, KFMB-TV and San Diego Police Museum)

As the rain continued to come down, raindrops can be seen on the lens of another TV news photographer who captured the photographer who had been at the car window getting his final shot as the four-hour standoff was now over.

(Courtesy KGTV, KFMB-TV and San Diego Police Museum)

(Courtesy KGTV, KFMB-TV and San Diego Police
Museum)

Spectators across the street, soaking wet from the rain
that continued to fall now talked among themselves about
what they had just seen and heard.

* * * * *

When Sergeant Brown walked to police chief Wesley Sharp's office, Sharp and a number of reporters met him. Brown recalled one of the reporters saying to Sharp, "Chief, your man is a hero" to which Sharp responded, "He's no hero. Any of my men would have done the same thing." Brown said when he heard that his first thought was "Then why the hell didn't they? Why did it have to be me?"

Brown spent the remainder of the day and night being interviewed by newspaper, radio, and television news reporters and anyone else who wanted to talk to him. He and his wife Vera were in the studios of KOGO-TV Channel 10 for their 11 P.M. news. The two finally made it home around midnight and after downing a large glass of vodka, Brown resigned himself to try and get a few hours of sleep. He wasn't given the next day off, in fact, he had to be back to work at 3 A.M. Sleep never came as Brown re-lived the entire incident over and over again in his mind. Three hours later Brown was in uniform and at work. Stress leave for officers involved in traumatic encounters was still years in the future.

Chapter 8
The Television Interviews

The night of the Hub shootout and the next day, television stations featured interviews with people who were in the middle of the firefight and standoff. KFMB-TV and KOGO-TV featured special reports during their regularly scheduled newscasts. When compared with newspaper stories of the incident, accounts occasionally differed, but there was no denying that pictures, both still and moving overpowered any word description.

A report the night of April 8, thirteen hours after the Hub shootout began, was aired on KOGO-TV, Channel 10 and anchored by Frank Van Cleave.

KOGO-TV news anchor Frank Van Cleave
(Courtesy KGTV and San Diego Police Museum)

(Courtesy KGTV)

The program's first interview was with eyewitness Tony Cido, a balding man in his late 50's or early 60's with short gray hair, who was a passerby right after Louis Richards was murdered.

(Courtesy KGTV and San Diego Police Museum)

Cido said, "I looked in the doorway and this man was lying with his face down and he was bleeding and his glasses were on the sidewalk. I heard him call police and I looked down at him and I looked in the store and I saw this man with his back towards me.

"So I went to the William Penn Hotel, which is right next-door, and I asked the desk clerk to call the police because there was a man that was shot. And I was going to get in my car at that time. I thought it would be best to get under cover, of which I did. And it must have been a few minutes later when the police arrived."

* * * * *

Then, although this newscast was on KOGO-TV, Channel 10, the station aired a filmed interview that had been done by KFMB-TV, Channel 8's Mel Knoepp who was the co-host for Channel 8's morning news and talk program Sun Up.

(Courtesy KFMB-TV)

(Courtesy KFMB-TV)

Having just gotten off the air, Knoepp was one of many at the station who headed downtown to report on the shootout.

Fifty-three years later, Knoepp, 84, speaking by telephone from his home near San Diego where he lives with his wife, Mary, remembers hearing the action on the police radio and going to the scene six blocks away with a camera crew.

In a clear, deep voice, much the same as he sounded on the air, he remembers bullets flying in both directions.

"We recorded a narration from the sidewalk near the store entrance," he said, "and we got a whiff of the tear gas the police used to try and flush the suspect out. We ran the story on the evening news and sent a copy of the report to the CBS Evening News. Walter Cronkite used about 12 seconds of it."

Most likely Channel 10 had a cameraman nearby at the scene and without a reporter, filmed Knoepp interviewing Navy Gunner's Mate Third Class, Frank Morales for their story.

(Courtesy KFMB-TV, KGTV and San Diego Police Museum)

The interview was filmed after Morales had tossed in the first hand grenade, but before he threw in the second.

Knoepp: "What's your name?"

Morales: "Morales, Frank W.—work with the shore patrol headquarters here in San Diego."

Knoepp: "You're the man who threw in the concussion grenade. What is the purpose of the concussion grenade? What do you expect it to do?"

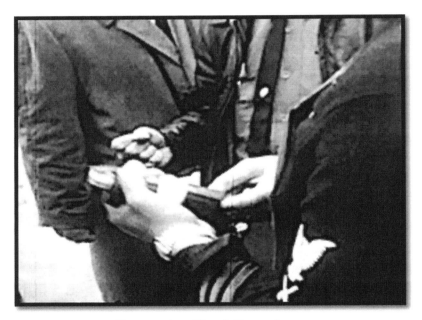

Concussion Hand Grenade
(Courtesy KGTV, KFMB-TV and San Diego Police
Museum)

Morales: "Well, they can make a hole in the brick wall there and knock a man off his feet. If he's protected, well, it won't hurt him. But if he's not protected it will kill him or knock him down."

Knoepp: "They think he's up now from where he was before the second floor mezzanine."

Morales: "Right. They think he's up on the second deck. And as soon as police give me some cover, I'll try to come up there and lob the hand grenade."

Knoepp: "This thing you're wearing." (Knoepp taps Morales on his chest)

(Courtesy KFMB-TV, KGTV and San Diego Police
Museum)

Morales: "It's a bulletproof vest. It'll just stop the bullet
here. And if he don't shoot at my head, I'll be alright."

* * * * *

More than two hours into the standoff, with gunfire
continuing in the background, Knoepp interviewed Carl
Davis. It was another interview done by a competing
station's reporter and shot by a Channel 10 photographer.

(Courtesy KFMB-TV, KGTV and San Diego Police
Museum)

Knoepp: "What's the difficulty? Why can't you get to him?"

Davis: "He's standing behind a concrete pillar and we can't get any shots to hit him."

Knoepp: "You've lobbed some tear gas shells in there. Why haven't they been effective?"

Davis: "He seems to be getting fat on 'em. That's the only thing I can say. It's not doing a bit of good to him."

Knoepp: "Is there a possibility he has a gas mask?"

Davis: "It's a possibility. We've never seen him."

Knoepp: "This has been going on for two hours and 15 minutes." (Davis looks at his wristwatch.)

(Courtesy KFMB-TV, KGTV and San Diego Police Museum)

"How many rounds of ammunition have you fired into that building?"

Davis: "I couldn't guess. I wouldn't have any idea."

Knoepp: "Hundreds?"

Davis: "In the hundreds."

Knoepp: "How many would you say he's answered back?"

Davis: "Oh, he pokes his head around the corner and fires every once in a while. When we first got here he fired four through the window at us. Just intermittent shooting. I don't know what he's shooting at now."

* * * * *

On KFMB-TV, Channel 8, reporter Harold Keen interviewed Theodore "Ted" Swienty, the clerk who got away and the lone survivor of the shootout. The ex-fishermen's face was weathered, his hair disheveled and he was wearing a dark sport coat with an open collar white shirt. He had some sort of pin on the left lapel of his coat and apparently was smoking a cigarette because the smoke kept wafting up during the interview. In a slow, low southern drawl, Swienty told what happened.

(Courtesy KFMB-TV and San Diego Police Museum)

Swienty: "Well, it happened so doggone fast. One minute I was selling him a gun and the next minute he grabbed a box of shells and took the gun and said I'm going to blast your (Swienty paused) brains out, you S.B. And that was it. The first shot, it's just my luck, the first shot he fired at Mr. Richards and I don't know, it seems the same time he turned and fired at him. I dropped behind the counter so I never even seen Mr. Richards after that.

Keen: "What did you do after dropping behind the counter?"

Swienty: "Well, I crawled off to the door and tried to make my escape out the mezzanine . . . up stairs . . . followed up on that and he come up behind me and fired a shot at me at the top of the stairs. So, instead of turning left, I turned to my right and tried to find a place to hide and managed to crawl under a bed.

(Swienty explains why the bed was upstairs.) Kept up (there) for relaxation and it was just my luck I wasn't found."

* * * * *

Keen then interviewed Inspector Wayne Colburn who was the officer in charge of the scene.

(Courtesy KFMB-TV and San Diego Police Museum)

Keen: "Inspector Colburn what were the problems that caused you to use such a wide variety of weapons and techniques?

Colburn: "Well, Harold we had two problems. We had first of all, we had a large number of personnel involved and acting on instructions from Chief Sharp, he advised me that he didn't want any heroics. He didn't want any officer hurt and we'd wait the man out. Second, in addition to the fact that we were not real familiar with the building."

* * * * *

The longest video record of the shootout was the special report that aired at the top of the eleven o'clock newscast that night on KOGO-TV. Frank Van Cleave was the news anchor and here is a transcript of the program:

Van Cleave: "As we have reported, the San Diego Police Department deserves a great deal of credit for the action they took today in San Diego during this four-hour gun battle. To single out one individual in the San Diego Police Department would not do justice to all of the men involved. We do have one man with us tonight, namely because he was involved in actually apprehending this suspect in the very final moments that played out the gun battle. He is Sergeant Allen Brown of the San Diego Police Department and with him is his wife, Mrs. Brown.

(Courtesy KGTV and San Diego Police Museum)

"Sergeant, we are very happy you could come by and give us some vivid descriptions of what happened today. We've now taken the action to the point where you are entering the store. What happened after that?"

Brown: "Just prior to entering, this Navy gunner's mate threw this concussion grenade into the store and it blew the glass out of the windows. I immediately rushed in followed by officer Augustine. We were carrying shotguns. We felt that the man was knocked unconscious and we wanted to get him before he came to.

"The inside was in complete shambles and there were several small fires started by the concussion grenade. And I rushed to the rear of the store and the man wasn't in sight and to the right was a room. I entered this room and couldn't see him and in a second room again off to my right. It was very dark and he could have been in there so I fired several rounds with the shotgun to wound him if he was in there and try to turn on some light so I could see him but there were no lights available. So we called for flashlights and then when the flashlights came I went and checked the room and he wasn't there. To my left was a staircase going up into the mezzanine. So I started up the mezza and the suspect fired at me and I came back down and told him if he didn't surrender to save his life that we were going to throw another grenade up there.

"So then I threw several packages of paper—written material up there later, hoping that he would hear this and surrender or fire or expose himself in some way or another, but he never made a move. So another concussion grenade was brought in and the gunner's mate threw this one up into the mezzanine and right after it went off I started up the stairs and he fired at me again. So I dropped back down the stairs and I fired several rounds through the ceiling trying to pinpoint his location so that we could get him from down below but we were unsuccessful.

"Then I heard him shouting and firing at officers out the window to the street and the officers were firing back so I went to the stairs and directly behind me was Sergeant Svidal who was off duty and heard of this incident and he covered in.

Lyder "Swede" Svidal
(Courtesy San Diego Police Museum)

"Behind officer Svidal was officer Augustine who had been with me throughout the entire operation and Lieutenant Clarence Myers who was right there with us. And I got up to the top and into the mezzanine that led to another door to my right. This was all heavily partitioned because this was why the second concussion grenade didn't get him.

Bob Augustine
(Courtesy San Diego Police Museum and Brown family)

Clarence Myers
(Courtesy San Diego Police Museum)

"I went in across the door and I looked back to my right and saw the suspect hiding behind the door with his pistol. I fired two rounds and I drove him from this area farther back and into a dark corridor and he fled about 15 feet and went to the right and ducked behind another partition.

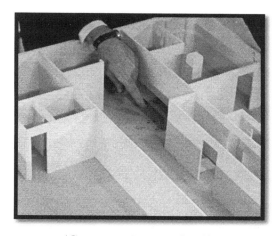

(Courtesy Brown family)

So I went after him and as I rounded the corner, there he was with a pistol in his hand and I had my shot gun in a ready position."

(The camera pulls back and shows Sergeant Brown making a motion with his hands as if he were holding a shotgun.)

(Courtesy of KGTV and San Diego Police Museum)

Brown: "I held the trigger back and I pumped the pump and they tell me I fired four rounds."

Van Cleave: "You weren't sure at the time?"

Brown: "It was that fast. I just emptied the gun on him. He was four feet from me."

* * * * *

In a *San Diego Union* report the next day, Sergeant Brown said after shooting the suspect, someone said there was someone else on the floor. Officers could hear heavy breathing in another room.

Brown said he asked the wounded Anderson, "Is there another man with you?" He got no answer.

Suddenly a voice called out. "I'm an employee. Don't shoot."

"I won't if you come out with your hands up," Brown answered.

Brown rushed into the other room and found Ted Swienty, the clerk for the Hub trying to get out from under a bed. Brown helped him.

Later when Brown returned to police headquarters, he learned the man he had shot was Robert Page Anderson, who had a record of narcotics arrests.

"I never saw him before," Brown said. "I never heard of him."

(The camera then shows Van Cleave, Brown and Brown's wife in the same shot. With light hair, Vera Brown was wearing a dark coat with some kind of bow on the right side and a scarf around her neck.)

(Courtesy KGTV and San Diego Police Museum)

(From the KGTV special report, news anchor Frank Van Cleave now spoke to Vera Brown.)

Van Cleave: "Mrs. Brown, your husband has been standing here giving us this intense description of an extreme danger that he faced this afternoon as a police officer in San Diego. Has he told you any of this before now? Have you heard any of the description he has given us?"

Vera Brown: "Yes, I heard it. We talked over it earlier this evening. He told me some of it. But I didn't hear it until late this afternoon."

Van Cleave: "What are your thoughts as a wife of a police officer? Do you realize that he's going to have to face danger like this?"

(Brown, dressed in a sport coat and narrow necktie of that era, looked at his wife with a smile.)

(Courtesy KGTV and San Diego Police Museum)

Vera Brown: "Yes and it's a worry each day, each time they go on duty. But you always feel that everything will be all right. They have their heart in it. He's happy and does a very good job and I know everything will be all right."

Van Cleave: "Sergeant and Mrs. Brown, thank you very much."

Brown: "Thank you."

(Van Cleave is then shown on a single shot standing on the set with a clock behind him. It is 11:17 P.M. just about 13 hours after the shooting at the Hub began.)

(Courtesy KGTV and San Diego Police Museum)

Van Cleave: "Incidentally, the Brown's have a son who is following the sergeant's footsteps. He is in police training."

* * * * *

(Allen Brown's son, Frank was a 21-year-old police
cadet the day of the shootout. He became a San Diego
police officer and was on the force four years before
enrolling in law school. He then became an attorney and
joined the San Diego County District Attorney's office
where he was a prosecuting deputy district attorney for 17
years. Following that, he was elected a judge in the San
Diego County Superior Court where he was on the bench
for 23 years. In 2018, Brown was 74, retired and living
with his wife, Maggie in the San Diego neighborhood of
Ocean Beach.)

Police Officer and Deputy District Attorney Frank Brown
(Courtesy Frank Brown)

Superior Court Judge Frank Brown   Frank Brown 2018
(Courtesy San Diego Police Museum)

On the day of the Hub shootout Frank Brown was at police headquarters on Market Street on the second floor in an academy classroom where officers in training were listening to radio accounts of the shootout. Believing his father had gone home after his nightshift, Brown was shocked when he heard radio accounts that his father was the officer who had shot the suspect.

(Courtesy Brown family)

Ever since he had first seen his father's police badge, Frank Brown wanted to become a cop. Eventually that dream was realized and during his four years as a cop, Brown's assignments included a beat in the same district where the Hub shooting took place.

Remembering April 8, 1965, after the standoff ended, Frank Brown said he went downstairs to the police coffee shop and there seated in a chair surrounded by other officers was his father.

"He was soaking wet," Brown remembers. "I went up to him, gave him a hug and told him 'I knew you could do it, dad. You always were bulletproof.'"

The next day Brown went to the Hub and walked where

his father had been.

"I saw a pool of blood on the second floor mezzanine where Anderson had fallen after my father had shot him," he said. Holding his hands together to create a large circle, he added, "And I saw the hole created when my father unloaded his shotgun into a door.")

* * * * *

KOGO-TV's report that night continued.

(Courtesy KGTV and San Diego Police Museum)

Van Cleave: "We've just checked County Hospital. The gunman has just come out of more than five hours of surgery. The hospital says he suffered a severe abdominal wound and arm wounds. He was conscious before he went into surgery but would not discuss the events of the day. He even refused to confirm that his name is Robert Anderson.

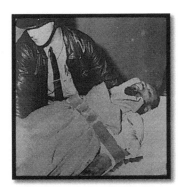

(Courtesy Steve Willard)

He will be charged with murder and attempted robbery if he lives. His condition remains critical.

"Until this moment, that is the story of todays shootout in San Diego, a gun drama which cost two lives and might cost a third and sent one San Diego policeman to the hospital and dozens of other police officers and innocent hostages in jeopardy of their lives, a drama seldom played out in San Diego and one which we hope will not be played out again."

(Courtesy KGTV and San Diego Police Museum)

(The clock on the set behind Van Cleave showed it was
11:17 P.M. a little more than 13 hours since the shootout
began.)

An announcer's voice then was heard speaking over
film of the shootout with white letters on the screen that
read SHOOTOUT IN SAN DIEGO.
"This has been Shootout in San Diego, a special report
on today's gun battle in downtown San Diego. This report
was brought to you by the three Southland Savings and
Loans—three of fifteen wholly owned subsidiaries of San
Diego Imperial Corporation.

(Courtesy KGTV and San Diego Police Museum)

"The film in this report was shot by Channel 10
cameramen Les Dodds, George Potter, Art Farian, Bob
Craft and Jack Moorhead.

(Courtesy KGTV and San Diego Police Museum)
Now stay tuned for more news."

* * * * *

Sergeant Allen Brown was the key person for news people to interview who covered the Hub shootout. In the following photo, Les Dodds is shown on the far left and to the right of Brown's shoulder in the center was veteran radio newsman Ed Deverill.

(Courtesy Brown family)

The next day, April 9 on KFMB-TV, Brown told reporter Harold Keen what happened after the second hand grenade was thrown.

(Courtesy KFMB-TV and San Diego Police Museum)

Brown: "Then he (Anderson) started firing out the window out front. I could hear officers shouting out then and shots going on . . . feeling that the suspect was distracted from me. I then went up the stairs again.

Sergeant Svidal was right behind me and Lieutenant Clarence Myers was behind him and officer (Bob) Augustine was behind him. We were just a mass of men going up the stairs. So I got up to the top of the stairs. I could hear the suspect. He moved off to my right behind the door. I fired two rounds with the shotgun into this door area and he fled down a narrow dark area and he fled down a narrow dark passageway then and disappeared to the right so I went after him and as I got down there it was much darker. I rounded the corner and he was standing there with a pistol in his hand and I emptied my shotgun at him at a range of about four feet."

* * * * *

The response from the media on this story was
instantaneous and considering that TV stations were using
film instead of videotape and that cell phones and other
communications devices were years in the future, coverage
of the Hub shootout was extremely professional. That is
not to say there were not moments of questionable news
judgment. One confirmed story is about KOGO-TV News
anchor Sam Rinaker, described by some as a "newsman's
newsman."

Sam Rinaker (tallest) with Regis Philbin on his right
(Courtesy KGTV)

On April 8, 1965, Rinaker was a member of the
downtown San Diego Rotary Club. Every Thursday their
meeting was a "must cover" event for Channel 10 to give
Rinaker a chance, as others put it, to "show off."

Sam Rinaker
(Courtesy KGTV)

Usually very little news came out of the meeting but coverage was mandatory. On the morning of April 8, Rinaker and KOGO-TV cameraman Art Farian were on their way from the TV station to the downtown meeting on Broadway.

Art Farian
(Courtesy Art Farian)

While driving there, the assignment desk diverted Rinaker and Farian to the shootout that was five miles from the TV station and a few blocks from the Rotary Club meeting. The pair arrived near Fifth and F and went to a nearby two-story building. Farian began filming out of a window using his silent camera and remembers Sergeant Allen Brown going to the front entrance and pulling the body of Louis Richards from the building.

After about 30 minutes of bullets flying, Rinaker turned to Farian and said, "I say, old boy, we need to go so we don't miss the meeting." They left and while Rinaker was probably basking in his glory with his fellow Rotarians, the firefight raged on for several hours. Quite likely the sound of rifles and machine guns from Fifth and F could be heard inside the meeting.

* * * * *

The following week on Wednesday, April 13, the Kiwanis Club at a Pillars of Freedom luncheon honored Police Inspector Wayne Colburn, Sergeant Allen Brown and Navy Gunner's Mate Third Class Frank Morales for "outstanding civic responsibility beyond the call of duty."

* * * * *

Art Farian was with KOGO-TV (later becoming KGTV) for 34 years and retired in 1994.

Art Farian
(Courtesy Bob Lampert)

In 2018, Farian, 90 divided his time between his hometown Fresno, California and a residence near San Diego in El Cajon, California.

(Courtesy Art Farian)

Chapter 9
The Images

Looking back more than fifty years, the still photos, video and sounds of what happened over four hours on April 8, 1965 at Fifth and F in San Diego are compelling. Having been in television news from 1969 to 2000, the stories I covered, including the six-day Los Angeles riots and the crash of an American Airlines DC-10 at O'Hare Airport in Chicago enable me to look at the visual accounts of the Hub shootout differently than most people. The images from that day, some lengthy and others brief; form a mosaic in understanding the story and appreciating what it took to record what happened. Taken individually, some may dismiss them as trivial and inconsequential. But woven together, they are threads that leave us with a remarkable example of photojournalism.

(Courtesy KGTV, KFMB-TV and San Diego Police Museum)

(Courtesy KGTV, KFMB-TV and San Diego Police
Museum)

The weather conditions during the shootout made it
difficult for police and news people to do their jobs. It
rained from start to finish. Sometimes it was a light
sprinkle but there were also extended periods where law
enforcement and the media were under torrential
downpours. The rainfall total for that day was 1.7 inches;
considerable since the normal rainfall for the entire season
in San Diego then was ten-and-a-half inches. The author
was told by several police officers that while the long one-
piece raincoat protected from the elements, it also covered
their revolvers and restricted access to their weapons.

For news people on April 8, just keeping the camera lens
clear of raindrops was a challenge as it was for officers to
avoid slipping on the wet pavement and sidewalks while
firing their weapons.

(Courtesy KGTV, KFMB-TV and San Diego Police
Museum)

(Courtesy KGTV and San Diego Police Museum)

One scene was especially intriguing. It showed a police officer in the pouring rain, kneeling next to his open driver's side door pointing his pistol across the front seat of the car and then shooting at the Hub through an open passenger window.

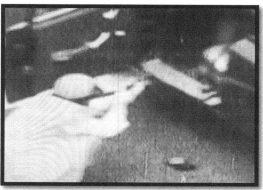

(Courtesy KGTV, KFMB-TV and San Diego Police Museum)

All through the morning and into the early afternoon, even though intersections around the scene were blocked, traffic signals continued to flash green, yellow, and red— green, yellow, red and pedestrians were advised to "Wait."

(Courtesy KGTV, KFMB-TV and San Diego Police Museum)

* * * * *

When newspaper editor Robert Crandall was carried over the shoulder of a man following his fatal heart attack, two women watched from the doorway of the William Penn Hotel, a decorative hanging flowerpot visible in the shot gave a stark contrast to the carnage in front of the women.

(Courtesy KFMB-TV and San Diego Police Museum)

Later it was reported that spectators jumped nervously
in unison when someone peering from a second-story
window accidently upset a flowerpot and sent it crashing
on the sidewalk with a loud plop.

(Courtesy KGTV, KFMB-TV and San Diego Police
Museum)

There are many scenes of Sergeant Brown shooting his rifle and shotgun. For a while, he strapped a large piece of metal to his chest to act as a bulletproof shield, but it was too heavy and restrictive so he discarded it.

(Courtesy KGTV, KFMB-TV and San Diego Police Museum)

In another shot Inspector Wayne Colburn is standing next to him as Sergeant Brown keeps pulling the trigger on his rifle and cartridges are ejected from the rifle, flying past an unconcerned Colburn.

(Courtesy KGTV, KFMB-TV and San Diego Police
Museum)

Reporters and police officers, including detective John
"Jack" Thompson, unsure when the gunman would open
fire, huddled where they could out of sight of Anderson.
For the Sparkletts bottled water company, there was free
advertising on television stations that night from a sign on
the back of the commandeered Coke truck.

Detective John "Jack" Thompson kneels near a charity receptacle bin.
(Courtesy KGTV, KFMB-TV and San Diego Police Museum)

The continuous shooting meant a need for fresh supplies of ammunition.

(Courtesy KGTV, KFMB-TV and San Diego Police
Museum)

(Courtesy Brown family)

All the while, people continued to crowd the scene a
block away on G Street.

Among the hundreds of onlookers, was 22-year-old Ron Moskowitz of San Diego. A few months away from beginning a 36-year career with the San Diego Fire Department, Moskowitz says he heard about the Hub shootout on the radio. In a telephone interview, Moskowitz, 76 talked about how he got close to the scene.

"I asked my cousin if she wanted to go down to see a shooting. She said she did so we made our way and after going through some alleys and buildings, we had a good spot to see things on Fifth Avenue."

When asked how he could get so close he said he knew the layout well from sneaking into downtown movie theaters as a kid.

(Courtesy KGTV, KFMB-TV and San Diego Police Museum)

    Video reports show surrounding businesses that are no longer there. Dave's Music Shop, the Porthole bar, Pacific Coastal Loans and the Singapore bar are all gone.

(Courtesy KGTV, KFMB-TV and San Diego Police Museum)

No longer there are Walker Scott Department Store, a girlie theater on the southwest corner of Fifth and F, and Dell Ray Tailors where sailors went. Services included "Blues cut down While u Wait" and "Alterations and Pressing WHILE-U-WAIT."

(Courtesy Brown family, KGTV, KFMB-TV and San Diego Police Museum)

On the side of the Hotel Horton was a painted sign for Caliente horse racing track in Tijuana and in front of that was the now defunct Boston Loans Company, a business that could easily have been chosen by Robert Anderson for his robbery.

(Courtesy KGTV, KFMB-TV and San Diego Police Museum)

* * * * *

As I watched the shootout video countless times, several questions went unanswered. Nothing of this magnitude had ever happened to the San Diego police and it was obvious those in charge were not quite sure how to bring the standoff to an end.

(Courtesy KGTV, KFMB-TV and San Diego Police
Museum)

It's likely that the Hub Loans & Jewelry Company's
owner, Sam Zelman called the police during the shootout
or was contacted by officers. You would think that he got
to the scene as quickly as possible and certainly would
have informed officers that he had two employees inside
his store. Louis Richards was known to have been killed
but Ted Swienty would have been somewhere in the store.

As it turned out, he was hiding under a bed in a second
floor room. So, the question remains: why did Sergeant
Brown fire his shotgun into the ceiling in an attempt to get
Anderson when Swienty might have been over the spot?

Other " whys" and "what ifs" are considered in Chapter
20.

Chapter 10
The Operation and Aftermath

Ninety minutes after Robert Anderson was shot, captured and put in a police ambulance, he was in a pre-surgery X-ray/recovery room five miles away at County Hospital in Hillcrest (now UCSD Medical Center).

Before a surgical team began working to repair massive gunshot wounds to both arms and his abdomen, they had to determine the extent of damage. In the photo that follows, a technician is positioning Anderson's left arm for an X-ray. Surgery would come later because the blanket that covered Anderson before he was placed in the ambulance is still in place along with two straps still secured to the gurney. Surgery would have been in a different sterile room with doctors and attendants wearing masks. It appears that blood from Anderson had soaked what he was lying on and there seems to be blood residue on the tile floor.

While an IV bag is hanging above Anderson's feet, there may be a blood bag with two lines visible behind a bag that is lettered REC ROOM that stood for Recovery Room.

An indication of the lax attitude when it came to cigarettes in hospitals is a sign in the room that reads NO SMOKING.

The clock on the wall shows 3:30 PM. The operation would not end until five hours later.

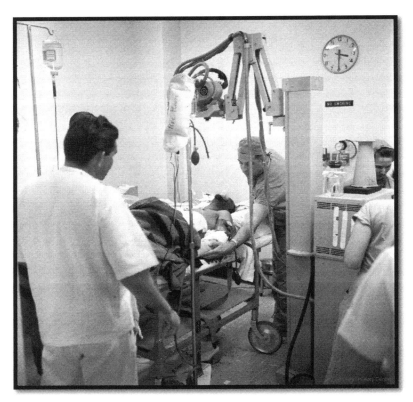

(Photo from San Diego History Center)

The next day, Fifth and F was the city's biggest sightseeing attraction. A stream of motorists drove by the Hub Loans & Jewelry Company and pedestrians flocked to where more than 65 police officers pumped as many as a thousand rounds of ammunition into the building during the four-hour gun battle with Robert Anderson who fired about a hundred shots in return.

On-lookers, sometimes up to 50 at a time, leaned over yellow police barricades to see what was visible through the shattered windows. Inside were bullet-riddled trunks each topped with cardboard boxes filled with clothing.

San Diego Union reporters Dick Bowman and Homer Clance reported that the Hub owner, Sam Zemen said that in addition to bullet holes, the clothing stank of tear gas.

Zeman said his store was insured "but I don't know if it covered anything as weird as this."

The tear gas police pumped into the store for several hours on Thursday was still strong enough inside the next day to burn the eyes, so firemen brought fans to ventilate the store. Glass from shattered display cases still littered the tile floor.

The newspaper account told of an electric guitar on the counter. It had been pawned shortly before the shootout began but now bullets had riddled it to splinters and blood was spattered on the guitar's gray case. Whose blood? Louis Richards had been shot and fell at the store's entrance but Ted Swienty had fled to avoid being shot. Could the blood have been Anderson's, cut from flying glass? No one was sure.

A *San Diego Union* story reported that people wondered about a blue aluminum trunk that was outside the store. Punctured with bullet holes, speculation came from an elderly woman wearing bobby socks who said, "I'll just bet that he hid behind that, wouldn't you know?"

A photo showed a detective examining a phonograph that had at least fifty bullet holes.

(Courtesy Brown family)

A sign behind the record players read UNREDEEMED WATCHES & DIAMONDS. And on a shelf along the wall were more than twenty suitcases. Below them was a gun case with rifles and pistols and in the middle of the photograph is what appears to be a sword in a sheath with a tag, possibly a pawned Navy officer's sword.

(Courtesy Brown family)

Ted Swienty was one of those at the shop the next day, looking at the devastation and remembering the horror of four hours hiding under a bed on the second floor.

He told reporters that police fired so many bullets into the shop "that slugs were rolling around me like marbles."

Swienty then pointed to a place on the loft wall and showed reporters were a shotgun blast had spattered flesh from the gunman's arm. Then he looked at a hole near his bed-hideout were a concussion grenade had blown out a wall.

Swienty and storeowner Sam Zemen walked around the
wrecked shop with an insurance adjuster, George Savage.

Once again, the Hub owner was asked about the
damage and said, "I can't begin to estimate the damage.
Am I insured? I hope so. But that's what we're here to see."

A *San Diego Union* story quoted Zemen's sister-in-law,
Lillian Zemen of La Mesa who also could not quantify the
financial loss involved. "My husband, Max, who owned
the store with Sam, his brother, died two years ago. So I
know how Mrs. Richards (the wife of the store manager
who was murdered) must feel."

"Mr. Richards was a faithful employee for 19 years,"
said Mrs. Zemen. "My heart goes out to his widow. What
a tragic waste of a good life. That crazy man with the gun.
I feel he'd be better off dead. He must have been under the
influence of drugs. What a senseless thing to do."

* * * * *

Outside display windows showed the aftermath of
hundreds of bullets fired into the F Street side of the
pawnshop. Ron Moskowitz, the young man who along
with his cousin got close to watch the shootout said he
returned to the scene a few days later. "There was hardly
anything inside that didn't have a bullet hole."

(Courtesy KGTV, KFMB-TV and San Diego Police Museum)

(Courtesy Brown family)
Sergeant Hugh French holds Sergeant Sam Chasteen's machine gun.

The next day was not without its oddities. The author was told that during the shootout an unidentified police captain positioned himself on a top floor of the building catty corner from the Hub for an unobstructed view. Armed with a bolt-action .30-06 caliber rifle and scope, he fired a single round into the pawnshop.

No one knows what he was firing at but later someone found the slug in an unusual place. The round had penetrated the walls separating Hub Loans from the adjacent William Penn Hotel to the east. The slug had just enough force to pierce the inner wall of the Penn elevator and without injuring anyone, dropped harmlessly to the elevator's floor.

* * * * *

An editorial in the *San Diego Union* the day after the shooting gave the newspaper's opinion on how the incident was handled. Headlined **Police Win Praise in Gun Battle**, the paper opined that, "The tragic gun fight in downtown San Diego yesterday was well handled by law enforcement officers.

"Bullets were flying for more than four hours, hostages were held, it was raining heavily at times, wind made tear gas ineffective and curious civilians presented a problem.

"Without discipline and skilled handling, the gun fight could have developed into a larger situation in which many more lives could have been endangered or lost.

"The leadership of the San Diego police who participated provided the cool determination and excellent judgment that kept loss of lives and injuries as low as possible.

"Commendations and thanks also are due the Navy personnel who assisted police in keeping the curious away as well as in bringing the gun battle to a conclusion.

"As in the past the Navy, like other military units in the area, showed cooperation, identification and rapport with the civilian community.

"It is hard to understand, however, the thoughtlessness of San Diegans who insisted on coming as close as possible to the shooting scene from curiosity. They interfered with effectiveness of the police and endangered their own lives.

"The gunfight was a tragedy of a type that is not typical in San Diego. It did show San Diegans, however, that their Police Department is among the best and thinks of duty before danger.

(Courtesy KGTV, KFMB-TV and San Diego Police Museum)

"They interfered with the effectiveness of police and endangered their own lives."

(Courtesy KGTV, KFMB-TV and San Diego Police Museum)

* * * * *

A week later, San Diego Police Chief Wesley Sharp commended his officers, giving personal commendations to 30 policemen and praising another 35 officers who were assigned to traffic control and handling a crowd of more than 1,000. One of those who received a commendation was Orv Hale, who pushed a gurney under the front window of the Hub to reach the body of Louis Richards.

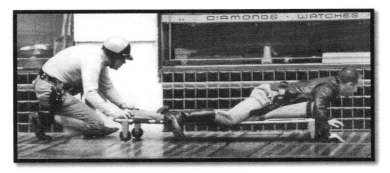

(Courtesy *San Diego Union* and San Diego Police Museum)

CITY OF SAN DIEGO · POLICE DEPARTMENT

DEPARTMENT COMMENDATION

Date __April 15, 1965__

Chief of Police:

On this date, it was my privilege to commend __Officer Orville M. HALE, Badge #904__

for the following reasons:

At the Hub Jewelry and Loan Company, 771 Fifth Avenue, April 8, 1965, during a four hour seige, this officer demonstrated outstanding ability to perform in keeping with the highest traditions of the law enforcement profession.

This officer is specifically commended for his courage in exposing himself to gunfire while assisting with the removal of the mortally wounded victim.

(Courtesy Orv Hale)

Chief Sharp also issued a written statement:

"My greatest concern was that no officers or innocent citizens were injured because of police carelessness. These instructions were given to Inspector (Wayne) Colburn who was in charge, and in my opinion performed an excellent job in carrying out these instructions."

Chief Sharp said the weather and the number of spectators created a particularly difficult situation.

"In my opinion, the officers conducted themselves in a commendable manner under extremely difficult circumstances," he said.

(Courtesy KGTV, KFMB-TV and San Diego Police Museum)

Chief Sharp said the gun battle was the biggest involving police during his 34 years on the force.

* * * * *

Police files showed that the closest thing to the standoff on April 8, 1965 was in April 1954, when a Linda Vista man barricaded himself in his home, set a trap and wounded five officers, one critically. It was estimated that police fired 25 shots.

The gunman, Barney Dennis opened up with a shotgun, critically injuring deputy marshal, Elwin Bunnell who was in the neighborhood serving papers on someone else.

Elwin Bunnell
(Courtesy San Diego Police Museum)

Also shot was detective John Zemcik who was wounded trying to save Bunnell. In the photo that follows, a nurse is treating Zemcik, while motorcycle officer John "Irish" O'Neal watches.

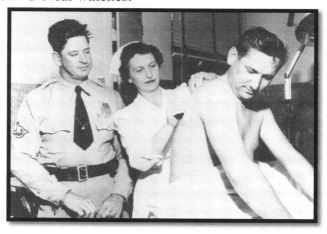

(Courtesy Steve Willard)

The gunman in the Linda Vista shootout, Barney Dennis was wounded but recovered to stand trial. Bunnell survived; however, after his recovery he could no longer perform his duties as a deputy marshal.

Chapter 11
The Trial

After the case against Robert Page Anderson was submitted to a grand jury, the suspect faced four felony charges. There was one count of murder in the death of Hub manager, Louis Richards; three counts of attempted murder of Hub employee Theodore Swienty and police officers William Duncan and Allen Brown; one count of the robbery of Theodore Swienty and Louis Richards; and one count of burglary at the Hub.

On April 12, 1965, Anderson was arraigned at County Hospital on the charges. Municipal Court Judge William T. Low advised Anderson of his rights, including the right to be represented by an attorney.

Judge William T. Low
(Courtesy San Diego County Judicial Services)

Anderson, who was on probation for marijuana possession told Judge Low that attorney Edgar Langford, represented him.

The judge then read the charges and set a preliminary hearing for May 7, and ordered Anderson held without bail.

Anderson objected when told news photographers wanted to take pictures prior to or after the proceedings. Hospital officials then denied photographers permission.

During the arraignment, the only thing Anderson requested was that he be allowed to sit up in bed—a request, which nurses denied.

San Diego Homicide Lieutenant Ralph Davis told reporters that Anderson, when interviewed had denied killing Hub manager Louis Richards and shooting at police officers.

Ralph Davis
(Courtesy KGTV, KFMB-TV and San Diego Police Museum)

Davis said Anderson told him a white masked bandit shot Richards but the suspect could not say what happened to the masked man when the shooting started.

Lieutenant Davis' response to that was, "We don't believe Anderson's story." Davis said Anderson, who was in critical condition from wounds in the abdomen and both arms was rambling while interviewed several times over the weekend after the shooting but was talking rationally.

Davis said that Anderson told detectives he went into the pawnshop to buy a suitcase and was confronted by a large white man wearing a mask. Anderson said that's when the shooting started and that the masked man did all the shooting in the shop. His story was that when he tried to help Richards the "masked man threatened him and that's why he didn't come out of the store." He claimed that he picked up a couple of guns to protect himself and one of them discharged. He repeated not knowing what happened to the masked man after the shooting started.

Davis said, "There is no indication that a masked bandit was present, and we're not going out looking for any masked bandit."

* * * * *

The trial was assigned to Department 9 of San Diego County Superior Court with Judge Verne O. Warner presiding. Anderson's court appointed defense attorney was 36-year-old James. J. Biggins, Jr. of the San Diego law firm Smith, Prante & Biggins.

James J. Biggins, Jr. 1962
(Courtesy Jutta Biggins)

The prosecuting attorneys were San Diego County
Deputy District Attorneys Robert Thomas and Gilbert
Smith.

Deputy District Attorney Robert Thomas
(Courtesy Brown family)

The 47-year-old Thomas was a native San Diegan, graduating from Hoover High School in 1936 and San Diego State College in 1943. After serving as a Naval officer in World War II and becoming an FBI agent, he was with the San Diego County District Attorney from 1954 to 1970 and became Chief Deputy District Attorney. In 1970 when District Attorney James Keller retired, Thomas ran for District Attorney but lost the election to United States Attorney Edwin L. Miller, Jr.

* * * * *

Because of his gunshot wounds, Robert Anderson was unable to make early court appearances. His preliminary hearing was on May 4, 1965 and a plea of not guilty was entered on his behalf. On June 2, 1965 a hearing was held in room 8 at San Diego County Hospital and Judge Verne Warner set the trial date for Tuesday, June 14, 1965.

On that day when Anderson was brought from the jail to Department 9, he walked into Judge Warner's courtroom with his arms in casts, the result of being wounded by Sergeant Brown.

(From Jet magazine)

A long-sleeved shirt partly covered the casts. A metal splint pin, cushioned by corks, protruded from Anderson's right hand. The pin could have been designed to keep small, shattered pieces of bone in place during the healing.

Kristin Burns, a registered nurse (RN) in San Diego expressed surprise to the author that Anderson's arm was not in a sling to keep it protected from being bumped and jarring the pin.

(Courtesy San Diego History Center)

Jury selection began with the court's clerk calling twelve people on the jury list and asking them to take a place in the jury box. Judge Warner made a brief statement explaining what kind of case was to be tried and then potential jurors were questioned about any reason they could not serve.

The process is known as voir dire (a French term meaning "to speak the truth"). Questions included such things as knowledge of the case, specific experiences they have had that might cause them to be biased or unfair and their thoughts about the death penalty. Each time a potential juror was dismissed for cause or from preemptory challenges given each side, a new person took a seat in the jury box.

Jury selection continued until the next day and just before noon on Wednesday, June 15, lawyers for Anderson and the District Attorney's office were satisfied with the selection. The panel of six men and six women with two women serving as alternate jurors were then sworn in.

Court Clerk George C. Wilken marked People's exhibits (evidence) 1 to 128 for identification only. The jury and the alternate jurors were admonished by the Court and excused for recess until 2 P.M.

At 2:07 P.M. the jury and alternate jurors returned into court. Dorothy Sloter took her position as the Court Reporter and used a stenotype machine to transcribe court testimony in shorthand.

The Court Clerk read the indictments of one count of murder; three counts of attempted murder and one count each of robbery and burglary against Robert Anderson to the jury. The People represented by Robert Thomas made an opening statement.

Anderson's attorney reserved his opening statement but later, James J. Biggins, Jr. would say that Anderson was given to "blind rages."

Theodore "Ted" Swienty, the clerk who escaped up the stairs from Anderson was the second witness to take the stand and would be the People's best witness about events leading up to the murder of Louis Richards, Swienty being shot at by Anderson and the four hours that followed.

Helping the jury understand the layout of the Hub
Loans and Jewelry Company was a scale model of the
building. In a photograph that follows, Sergeant Brown
and Deputy District Attorney Robert Thomas review the
model prior to the state presenting its case against Robert
Anderson. The mock-up of the Hub Loans & Jewelry
Company was 4 feet by 4 feet and stood about two feet
high. Sheriff's Deputy R.T. Nilson, who built it, testified
he was with county engineers when they measured the
store layout after the gun battle.

Deputy Nilson said he spent 94 hours constructing the
mock-up from plans drawn up by the engineers. The
model shows the Hub's layout and most importantly, the
second floor hallway where Ted Swienty fled and the
room where he hid.

In the photograph, Sergeant Brown points to where
Anderson was standing when the suspect misfired a pistol
at him and where Brown used his Winchester model .12-
gauge pump-action sawed-off shotgun, called by some "a
cop's best friend," to bring him down. The model also
shows how large the storage area was on the second floor
where additional weapons and ammunition were kept.

Allen Brown with Deputy District Attorney Robert
Thomas
                    (Courtesy Brown family)

    While he testified, Swienty referred to the model and
photos taken at the scene. Swienty said when store
manager Louis Richards summoned him into the store
from outside, the first thing he noticed when he saw
Anderson was that the suspect needed a shave. Swienty
testified that Richards mentioned something about 30-30
shells for Anderson, "but there was no mention of a gun at
that time."
    He testified that Anderson pointed to a .32-caliber
special in a gun case and said he thought it was a 30-30.

He said Anderson told him he intended to get a 30-30
and continued looking at the .32-caliber special.

"Then he pointed to a rifle with a scope on it," Swienty
said. "He asked what that was and I told him it was a 30.06
rifle.

"He asked to see it and I showed it to him. He then
examined the rifle, sighted down the scope and pulled the
bolt back, looking through the rifle.

"He mentioned how good the scope was and I told him
it was a good scope having been made in Germany."

The rifle then was shown to Swienty, who identified it.

The major parts of the People's exhibits, including the
model of the Hub were received in evidence. Exhibits
began with a 16x20 photograph of the F Street side of the
store and continued with photos throughout the store.
Evidence introduced later included many firearms,
ammunition and the Remington .30--.06 rifle, serial
#156719 with a telescopic sight attached that Anderson
had asked for when he went into the pawnshop and the
receipt #70707.

Personal affects of Anderson were also part of the
evidence including his cigarette lighter, a package of
Salem cigarettes, a bus transfer, $1.08 in change, right and
left-hand leather gloves, the blood-stained clothing he was
wearing and the diamond ring he had brought to the store,
supposedly to sell or pawn.

Ted Swienty was on the witness stand for the rest of the
day as all 128 exhibits were received in evidence. Court
was recessed until Wednesday, June 16th at 10:00 A.M
and the sequestered jury and two alternate jurors were
taken five miles north to the Mission Valley Inn hotel.

* * * * *

Looking back on news coverage of what happened April 8, 1965 and the weeks that followed, the news reports, while mentioning that Louis Richards, the manager of the Hub was killed, most attention focused on the shootout, details about the gunman, Robert Anderson and Sergeant Brown.

The most anyone learned about Louis Richards came from his brief obituary on April 9 and the office of the County Coroner, Robert L. Creason. In a report by Deputy Coroner, W.T. Souza, Richards' death was set at 10:10 A.M. April 8, the result of a 30.06 caliber rifle gunshot wound to his back at 771 Fifth Avenue in San Diego. Creason established identification of Richards' body at the Coroner's office the day of Richards' death, but an autopsy was not performed until the following day.

Dr. Robert R. Eggen, Chief Pathologist for the Coroner detailed his findings in a report submitted on April 13, 1965. He noted the presence of abrasions above and below the right eyebrow and a broken nose that would have been consistent with Richards falling face first in the doorway of the Hub after he was shot in the back. Dr. Eggen also noted a bullet wound exit on Richards' chest.

The examination of Richards' back revealed a perfectly circular gunshot entrance wound in the lower portion of his body below the rib cage. Dr. Eggen noted that on the back of Richards' left forearm was a tattoo.

Richards' body was opened with a routine "Y" incision. The skin around the exit wound was hemorrhaged while the interior abdominal area had extensive hemorrhaging. The path of the bullet and damage shows why Richards died shortly after being shot. The slug shattered bones, including the spine and disc before lacerating the left kidney and going through the pancreas before exiting the abdomen.

The technical cause of death was listed as "Intraperitoneal hemorrhage due to laceration of aorta due to gunshot wound of back."

Below that sentence were Dr. Eggen's signature, name and title.

* * * * *

In the days that followed, the jury heard about the arsenal of weapons and ammunition at the Hub Loans & Jewelry Company. Criminologist Wayne Burgess, one of three police investigators called to the stand, said two pistols and ten rifles showed evidence of having been fired. He said 50 empty rounds of ammunition were found at the pawnshop following the four-hour shootout. Burgess testified that tests on the ammunition showed that most of it was fired from a .38-caliber weapon found after Anderson was shot by a policeman.

Burgess said there were no fingerprints on the weapons, but another officer, Detective Kenneth J. O'Brien, said Anderson was wearing a black glove on his left hand when he was shot, and another glove of the same type, for the right hand was found on the floor.

Kenneth O'Brien
(Courtesy S.D.P.O.A)

As was the case for news reporters, Sergeant Allen Brown captivated the jury with his account of what happened the afternoon of April 8.

(Courtesy Brown family)

Just as he had done in written and televised reports,
Sergeant Brown made the jurors feel that they were with
him every harrowing step of the way from the moments he
arrived on the scene to when he entered the store and then
the final confrontation when he shot Anderson.

* * * * *

On Monday, April 21, 1965 after the prosecution rested
its case, the defendant, Robert Anderson took the witness
stand. He gave a rambling and sometimes confusing
account of the incident that included his claim that he was
subjected to racial slurs when he first went into the
pawnshop. Anderson said he was hospitalized at one time
for meningitis, but under cross-examination admitted that
he had not been treated during he last ten to 12 year.

He testified that he blacked out temporarily when the
pawnshop manager Louis Richards was shot to death.
Anderson admitted doing all of the shooting that came out
of the Hub Loans and Jewelry Company. When asked
about exchanging shots with an officer creeping toward
the door he claimed he fired over the officer's head and
not at him.

That officer was 31-year-old Detective William Duncan
who exchanged gunfire as he crept toward the open front
door entrance at the beginning of the four-hour shootout.
He was one of three named in Anderson's attempted
murder charges.

Detective William Duncan
(Courtesy San Diego Police Museum)

Anderson testified that he had gone downtown on April 8 to see a movie. He also said that he bought a Derringer pistol in another pawnshop. He said he was convicted in 1962 on a narcotics violation and knew it was illegal for an ex-convict to possess firearms, but thought the Derringer was more of an antique than a weapon.

On his way to the movie he walked by the Hub store and wondered whether he could get "a good deal" by exchanging his diamond ring for a rifle.

"They (Richards and Swienty) talked kind of funny," Anderson said. "Like they didn't want to serve me."

He said Swienty agreed to take the ring in exchange for a rifle, but made statements such as "it's just like your kind of people."

"It made me pretty mad," said Anderson. "I've been mad before, but not like that."

He testified that he recalled asking for ammunition for the rifle, a 30-06 caliber, and seeing Swienty place it on the counter.

Anderson said he picked up the rifle, and that the next thing he knew he was stooping over the "dead man."

He didn't remember chasing Swienty up a flight of stairs to an upstairs storage room but said he "trotted" after Swienty to ask him what had happened and denied saying he would "blow your brains out" to Swienty just before Richards was shot.

He gave no reason why he did not give himself up when police asked him to.

* * * * *

Anderson's claims brought about rebuttal witnesses. One of them, Dr. Carl E. Lengyel, a psychiatrist was called by the prosecution and said that it was "absolutely impossible" for Anderson to have suffered a "momentary" epileptic seizure and then hold off police in a four-hour gun battle as claimed by the defendant's defense.

He and two psychologists also testified that a June 17 electroencephalogram (a machine that tests brain waves) administered to Anderson gave no indication of abnormalities as testified by defense expert witnesses called two days earlier.

Dr. Lengyel said he ruled that on the basis of the brain wave test and the defendant's medical history there was no evidence of organic brain impairment or epilepsy.

Dr. Charles W. Sult, Jr., a psychologist, testified than after interpreting the June 17 test, he found no indications of abnormalities and nothing to indicate that Anderson was not functioning as a completely normal person during the incident.

* * * * *

Final arguments from prosecutor Robert L. Thomas began on Friday, June 25 who urged the jury to convict Anderson of first-degree murder.

Anderson's court-appointed attorney James, J. Biggins, Jr. followed and urged for a verdict of at worst, second-degree murder based on testimony he said showed Anderson had a history of epilepsy and that he blacked out at the time of the murder.

James J. Biggins, Jr.
(Courtesy Utta Biggins)

(In a court document filed by Biggins in support of a motion for pretrial discovery, Biggins wrote that after his client's arrest and when he was in custody, Anderson "made statements to persons whose identities are unknown to him when he was mentally and emotionally upset and disturbed, and suffering from grievous physical wounds; he is informed and believes that said persons were law enforcement agents of San Diego City and/or County, medical and psychiatric personnel, acting at the behest of the San Diego Police Department or the San Diego County

District Attorney's office; that he is presently unable to recall all that he said and cannot fully inform me about the contents of such statements, and therefore all notes, reports and recordings relating to said statements are necessary to refresh defendant's memory and recollection.

Biggins also requested "A determination of the presence or absence of drugs or narcotics in the defendant's system, and his psychiatric or emotional condition, prior to and during the events complained of, and after his arrest, are necessary for preparation of the defendant's case . . . ")

Prosecution medical experts testified it would have been impossible for Anderson to suffer a momentary seizure as he claimed and then engage in the four-hour gun battle.

That same day after closing arguments were concluded, Judge Warner read instructions to the jury that included a mandate to reach verdicts on charges against Anderson of murder, attempted murder, robbery and burglary. If the decision were first-degree murder, jurors would then have to decide the penalty: death in San Quentin's gas chamber or life in state prison.

It was then time to submit the case to the six-man, six-woman jury. Once in the jury room, the members chose William Randolph Gibson as foreman and began deliberations.

The jury returned to court at 5 P.M. to rehear definitions of first-degree murder, attempted murder, robbery and burglary. Soon afterward, Judge Warner allowed the sequestered jury and two alternate jurors to go to dinner and then they were taken by bus to the Mission Valley Inn for the weekend with deliberations set to resume Monday morning.

When the weekend was over, the jury and two alternate jurors returned to court at 8:20 A.M. to further consider their verdict. At 10:12 A.M., after nine hours of deliberation the jury reached a decision. It was submitted in writing and signed by the Foreman, William Randolph Gibson.

 (TITLE OF COURT & CAUSE) VERDICT NO. CR. 8039
We, the jury in the above and entitled cause, find the defendant, ROBERT PAGE ANDERSON, Guilty of the crime of Murder as charged in Count One of the Indictment and fix the degree thereof as Murder in the First Degree.
Dated: - June 29, 1965.

WILLIAM RANDOLPH GIBSON
Foreman
and

We, the jury in the above and entitled cause, find the defendant, ROBERT PAGE ANDERSON, Guilty of the crime of Attempted Murder as charged in Count Two of the Indictment.
Dated:- June 28, 1965

WILLIAM RANDOLPH GIBSON
Foreman
and

We, the jury in the above and entitled cause, find the defendant, ROBERT PAGE ANDERSON, Guilty of the crime of Attempted Murder as charged in Count Thee (SIC) of the Indictment.
Dated:- June 28, 1965

WILLIAM RANDOLPH GIBSON
Foreman

and

We, the jury in the above and entitled cause, find the defendant, ROBERT PAGE ANDERSON, Guilty of the crime of Attempted Murder as charged in Count Four of the Indictment.
Dated:- June 28, 1965

WILLIAM RANDOLPH GIBSON
Foreman

and

We, the jury in the above and entitled cause, find the defendant, ROBERT PAGE ANDERSON, Guilty of the crime of Robbery as charged in Count Five of the Indictment and fix the degree thereof as First degree.
Dated:-June 28, 1965

WILLIAM RANDOLPH GIBSON
Foreman

and

We, the jury in the above and entitled cause, find the defendant, ROBERT PAGE ANDERSON, not guilty of the crime of Burglary, as charged in Count Six of the Indictment.
Dated:- June 28, 1965

WILLIAM RANDOLPH GIBSON
Foreman

The verdicts are again read as recorded. At the hour of 10:21 A.M. the jury and the alternate jurors are admonished by the Court and excused until Wednesday, June 30th, 1965 at 10:00 A.M.

MINUTES DEPT 9 DATE June 29th, 1965
* * * * *

Based on the dates of each verdict, it was apparent the jury made their decisions on the lesser charges before reaching agreement on the murder charge.

Not mentioned in the reading of the verdicts were the victims; Louis Richards, the Hub manager murdered, Sergeant Allen Brown, Hub clerk Ted Swienty, and Detective William Duncan the three men Anderson was convicted of trying to murder, and Louis Richards and Ted Swienty who were robbed.

The not guilty verdict on the burglary charge came after jurors were unable to agree that a theft had occurred at the Hub.

* * * * *

As each verdict was read, Anderson, seated at a table with his attorney showed no emotion. His arms remained in casts, the result of being shot by Sergeant Brown before he was captured.

(Courtesy San Diego History Center)

The following day, the jury reported to Department 9 to begin the penalty phase of the case. Their decision was to fix the penalty at death for the murder of Louis Richards.

* * * * *

Court documents provide insight on Robert Anderson. After a description of the weapons introduced into evidence, the "Views and Recommendations" prior to the penalty phase of the trial are as follows:

"This case was an extremely aggravated killing of a clerk in a pawnshop without justification or provocation. The defendant, after killing his victim, single-handedly then engaged in a four-hour pitched battle with sixty officers of the San Diego Police Department, endangering officers and various citizens.

An insight into the defendant's attitude is reflected on page 2 of the probation report, which is as follows:

"Anderson was interviewed . . . in the San Diego County Jail on July 9, 1965. At that time Anderson acknowledge (SIC) his guilt in the crimes and narrated the details in an unemotional manner. When asked what his attitude was, he replied, 'bitter.' His main line of thought seemed to be that he could have killed a lot more people but refrained from doing so only to have the 'authorities' order the death penalty for him. He then expressed the wish that he had killed some other people as long as the verdict turned out as it did.

"It should be noted that the defendant was previously granted probation in 1962 for possession of marijuana, at which time a thorough and complete psychiatric work-up was done on the defendant. At that time he was found to be a sociopath with a hostile personality, with a high delinquency potential with a poor prognosis following discharge, and that he was hostile and aggressive to society.

"In the event that this matter should be reversed for some reason as to the penalty phase, and the penalty reduced, it is the suggestion of the writer that the defendant should serve <u>life</u> in <u>prison.</u> (Author's note: the words "life in prison" are underlined on the original court document.)

* * * * *

The State then went about the process of setting dates of execution. On July 21, 1965, San Quentin Warden Lawrence E. Wilson sent a letter to Judge Warner regarding Robert Page Anderson, now with the prisoner number A91287.

Notice the bureaucratic and almost antiseptic tone of the letter that was part of the routine involving inmates in line for their reserved seat in the gas chamber.

STATE OF CALIFORNIA—YOUTH AND ADULT CORRECTIONS AGENCY   EDMUND G. BROWN, Governor

DEPARTMENT OF CORRECTIONS
CALIFORNIA STATE PRISON
SAN QUENTIN, CALIFORNIA 94964

FILED

JUL 22 1965

R. B. JAMES, Clerk

BY _____ DEPUTY

July 21, 1965

Re: ANDERSON, Robert Page
#A91287
(Condemned)

Hon. Verne O. Warner, Judge
Superior Court of San Diego County
San Diego, California.

Dear Judge: SETTING DATES OF EXECUTION
                 Superior Court Case No: CR-8039

We wish to acknowledge receipt of the inmate referred to
above from your county under sentence of death.

Because of the increased number of prisoners under sentence
of death, it would be of considerable assistance if you
would contact my office before a date of execution is set
by your court so that we might apprise you of any other
executions scheduled for that general time. In this way we
hope to avoid any possible conflicts that might arise with
other schedulings.

The California Supreme Court has suggested that there be no
executions on Friday, if possible, because of its schedule.
Also, as it is necessary for us to make preparations the day
before the execution, we prefer not to have them on Monday.
We suggest, therefore, that the days of Tuesday, Wednesday,
or Thursday, be used.

Assuring you of our continued cooperation in handling these
problems to the best interest of all concerned, I remain

Sincerely yours,

LAWRENCE E. WILSON, Warden

LEW/Vs.

cc District Attorney (trial county) James Don Keller

cc County Clerk ...., James, Attn: Merritt W. Smith,

Chapter 12
The Appeals

Up to this point, the trial, verdicts and penalty phase had played out with no complications. Anderson was sent to the California Institute for Men at Chino, California while the automatic appeal process began under section 1239b of the California Penal Code, which provides that after a death sentence, the case is automatically appealed to the State Supreme Court.

But then a decision on May 24, 1966 set in motion events that would have massive legal repercussions in the years to come. Included in the narrative printed below are some of the reasons Anderson was found not guilty of burglary at the Hub Loans & Jewelry Company. (Note: there are several typographical errors in the court document including the name of one of the officers is misspelled. McClennon should be spelled Mclennan. And the wrong date is given. April 18, 1965 should be April 8, 1965.)

Supreme Court of California, In Bank.

The PEOPLE, Plaintiff and Respondent, v. Robert Page ANDERSON, Defendant and Appellant.

Cr. 9317.

Decided: May 24, 1966

Rufus W. Johnson, San Bernardino, under appointment by the Supreme Court, for defendant and appellant. Thomas C. Lynch, Atty. Gen., William E. James and Albert W. Harris, Jr., Asst. Attys. Gen., S. Clark Moore, Edward P. O'Brien and Michael R. Marron, Deputy Attys. Gen., for plaintiff and respondent.

This is an automatic appeal (Pen.Code, s 1239, subd. (b)) from a judgment, after trial before a jury, on verdicts finding defendant guilty of (a) murder of the first degree, (b) attempted murder of three men, and (c) robbery of the first degree, and imposing the death penalty.

Facts: About 10 a.m. on April 18, 1965 (SIC should be April 8, 1965), defendant entered a pawnshop in San Diego attended by two employees, Theodore Swienty and Louis Richards. He had less than $2 in cash and a diamond ring on which he still owed approximately $60 on a conditional sales contract and for which he realized he could obtain only about $10 cash.

Defendant first asked for .30—.30 ammunition, and when Swienty informed him that he had none, defendant inquired about some rifles on display. At defendant's request, Swienty removed from its case a Remington .30—.06 with a telescopic sight attached and handed it to defendant for inspection. After examining the gun, defendant asked its price and was told it was $105. Defendant remarked that the price was quite steep, but declared, 'I'll take it.' He then asked for a box of shells, which Swienty procured and placed on the counter with the gun.

While Swienty was totalling the price of the two items, defendant reached over and seized the gun and ammunition. When Swienty protested, defendant said he wanted to see if the shells fit and started loading the gun as he backed away from the counter. Swienty moved toward defendant, but halted when he heard the rifle bolt slam shut and found himself staring into the barrel of the gun. Pointing the loaded rifle at Swienty from point blank range, defendant said, 'I'm going to blow your brains out, you son of a bitch.'

The other salesman, Richards, said to defendant: 'If you want it, you can have it. Take it and go.' As defendant swung the gun away, Swienty ducked for cover below the counter and heard Richards exclaim, 'Don't shoot,' followed almost immediately by a rifle blast.

A passer-by, Antonio Cidot, witnessed the murder. He heard the rifle blast and saw Richards fall to the floor, face down, near the open doorway of the pawnshop.

After the fatal shot was fired, Swienty came from behind the counter where he had taken refuge and ran up some stairs to another portion of the shop. As he reached the top of the stairs, he heard another shot fired in the room behind him. He then ran through the upstairs storage rooms to the front of the building, opened a window, and shouted for the police.

Hearing footsteps on the stairs, Swienty fled to the rear of the building and hid under a bed in a small, darkened room. He heard someone walking stealthily within a few yards of his hiding place and heard him mutter, in a voice which he recognized as that of defendant, 'He ain't here. Son of a bitch.'

The footsteps retreated, and for the next four hours, as he lay beneath the bed, Swienty heard shots fired from within and without the building, and heard several calls from the street advising defendant to come out of the shop with his hands up. He also heard both the explosion of grenades and shotgun blasts within the shop, and suffered from the tear gas used by the police.

Officer McClennon (SIC), of the San Diego Police Department's burglary detail, arrived on the scene and, hearing that defendant had a gun, immediately took cover nearby. From his vantage point, he observed Officer Duncan edging toward the door of the pawnshop with handgun drawn. He could also see the victim on the floor, and saw defendant inside carrying a rifle with a telescopic sight and moving toward the doorway.

Officer McClennon (SIC) saw defendant stop as Officer Duncan moved to the entrance of the pawnshop. When the two men confronted each other, defendant raised his rifle and fired at Duncan. Duncan fired back; both men then retreated, neither apparently having been hit.

Sergeant Allen Brown, of the San Diego Police Department, made several appeals over a loudspeaker, encouraging defendant to surrender. No response was made to any of these appeals, and the intermittent firing from within the building gave no indication of any intention on defendant's part to surrender.

When both tear gas and concussion grenades failed to flush defendant from the building, Sergeant Brown, in company with other officers, finally entered the shop while sporadic gunfire was coming from within and proceeded toward the rear staircase. As Brown started up the stairs, a shot rang out from the vicinity of the top of the stairs, travelling in his direction. He retreated and shouted to defendant that another concussion grenade would be thrown and advised him to surrender to save his life.

After the grenade was thrown, the sergeant began to work his way up the stairs. Once again a shot rang out, this time quite close to him. He retreated, and then started back up the stairs. As he reached the top, he heard a metallic click, which sounded like a trigger, and, looking in the direction of the sound, saw defendant crouched with a pistol in his hand in a nearby darkened room. He pursued defendant to a rear storage area, where he felled him with a shot and apprehended him.

Defendant was wearing an empty gun belt, and on the floor beneath him were two handguns. Several rifles, a shotgun, and other handguns were found strewn about both the main part of the shop and the upper floor. These weapons had previously been in their proper storage cases; defendant had smashed the top of a glass storage case to obtain the handguns. The murder weapon was recovered on the second floor, and various types of live and expended ammunition were found on both floors.

Several large denomination keys had been depressed on the cash register. Before the murder the last cash register transaction had been $3, and the large denomination keys had not been depressed that day prior to the shooting.

Defendant admitted he saw Swienty run up the rear staircase of the shop and admitted following him; he admitted punching the cash register keys in an attempt to

break in and obtain money; he admitted shooting the box
of ammunition taken with the murder weapon, taking rifles
from the racks on the second floor, and breaking into the
glass pistol case; and he admitted firing at Officer Duncan,
but said he did not attempt to hit him but was, rather,
trying to keep him from entering the pawnshop.

Questions: First. Was the evidence sufficient to support the
robbery conviction?

Yes. From the evidence, the jury could reasonably have
found that when defendant entered the pawnshop, he had
no intention of purchasing a rifle and ammunition; that
once the salesman had produced the desired weapon and
ammunition, he took both items without ever having made
an offer to pay for them; that when the salesman sought
the return of the rifle and the ammunition, he loaded and
aimed the weapon at the clerk and threatened him; that in
fear of his life, the salesman stopped his attempt to retrieve
the merchandise, ducked behind the counter when
defendant swung the rifle away from him, and fled up the
back steps after the fatal shot at Richards; and that when
Richards told defendant he could have the rifle without
payment and then pleaded with him not to shoot, he was
murdered by a bullet from that same rifle.

Defendant contends that since he obtained possession of
the rifle without the use of force or fear, there can be no
robbery as a matter of law.

In this state, it is settled that a robbery is not completed at
the moment the robber obtains possession of the stolen
property and that the crime of robbery includes the
element of asportation, the robber's escape with the loot
being considered as important in the commission of the
crime as gaining possession of the property. (People v.

Ketchel, 59 Cal.2d 503, 523(10), 30 Cal.Rptr. 538, 381
P.2d 394; People v. Kendrick, 56 Cal.2d 71, 90(18), 14
Cal.Rptr. 13, 363 P.2d 13; People v. Phillips, 201
Cal.App.2d 383, 385—386, 19 Cal.Rptr. 839; People v.
Reade, 197 Cal.App.2d 509, 512(3), 17 Cal.Rptr. 328.)

Accordingly, if one who has stolen property from the
person of another uses force or fear in removing, or
attempting to remove, the property from the owner's
immediate presence, as defendant did here, the crime of
robbery has been committed.

In People v. Phillips, supra, 201 Cal.App.2d 383, 19
Cal.Rptr. 839, the defendants drove into a gasoline station
with the intention of committing a robbery. The plan was
for one of them to order gasoline and detain the attendant
at the car, while the other was to pretend to go to the men's
room but actually enter the service station and seal (SIC)
the contents of the cash box.

After the attendant had pumped gasoline into the tank, the
defendant in the car confronted him with a rifle, saying,
'Move and your dead.' The attendant, in spite of the
threats, upon seeing the other defendant rummaging in the
office, ran around the back of the car into the office, where
a struggle took place. The robber broke loose, and he and
his companion drove away, with the attendant calling out
to them that they owed $2.98 for the gasoline. They were
subsequently charged with robbery for the taking of the
gasoline.

Admittedly, no force or fear had been used by the robbers
in obtaining possession of the gasoline; the threats, the
display of the rifle, and the struggle with the attendant all
took place after the transfer of the gasoline to the car. The
contention was made that there could therefore be no

robbery as a matter of law; but the court affirmed the
judgment of conviction, finding no difficulty in upholding
the implied finding of the jury that under the
circumstances the gasoline was removed from the
immediate presence of the attendant by means of force and
fear, in violation of section 211 of the Penal Code.

Second. Did the trial court commit prejudicial error by
failing to instruct the jury, on its own motion, as to the
requisite force or fear necessary to constitute the crime of
robbery?

No. Defendant complains that the court committed
prejudicial error in failing to instruct on 'requisite force'
and the 'legal connotation of fear' as necessary elements
of the crime of robbery. He does not, however, challenge
the content of the robbery instructions given, nor did he
request any additional instructions at the trial.

Defendant's contention essentially is that the instructions
given needed amplification or explanation; but since he
did not request such amplification or explanation, error
cannot now be predicated upon the trial court's failure to
give them on its own motion. (People v. Reed, 38 Cal.2d
423, 430(1), 240 P.2d 590; People v. Shepherd, 223
Cal.App.2d 166, 173(4), 35 Cal.Rptr. 497.)

In the present case, the court properly instructed the jury
on the general principles of law governing the count of the
indictment charging defendant with robbery.

The law is settled that when terms have no technical
meaning peculiar to the law, but are commonly understood
by those familiar with the English language, instructions as
to their meaning are not required. (Cf. People v. Chavez,
37 Cal.2d 656, 668(6), 234 P.2d 632; People v. Chapman,

207 Cal.App.2d 557, 578(22), 24 Cal.Rptr. 568; People v. Sanderson, 190 Cal.App.2d 720, 723, 12 Cal.Rptr. 69.)

The terms 'force' and 'fear' as used in the definition of the crime of robbery have no technical meaning peculiar to the law and must be presumed to be within the understanding of jurors.

Third. Did the trial court abuse its discretion by not furnishing the jury with written instructions?

No. Defendant recognizes that furnishing written instructions is a matter within the discretion of the trial court, but urges that in capital cases it should be declared mandatory, upon either the motion of the defendant or the expressed need of the jury, that the jury be given written copies of the instructions to have with them in the jury room.

There is no merit to this contention. Section 1093 subdivision 6, of the Penal Code provides, in pertinent part: 'The trial judge May cause copies of instructions so given to be delivered to the jurors at the time they are given.' (Italics added.)

At the time the instructions were given, no request was made to furnish written copies to the jurors. The first mention of this question came almost six hours after the conclusion of the court's instructions and after the jury had deliberated for some time. Then the jury foreman merely asked, 'Are the written instructions available to the jury?' The matter was then discussed by court and counsel in the judge's chambers.

In denying defendant's motion that the jury be furnished written instructions, the court stated that written copies of the instructions exactly as given were not readily available, since they existed only in the court reporter's untranscribed notes, that the amount of time required for transcription was not available, and that the court felt it not advisable to furnish written instructions.

In informing the jury that the written instructions were not available, the trial court offered to reread any instructions the jury might request; and, in fact, the court did reread several of the instructions to the jury.

Clearly, the court did not abuse the discretion granted it under section 1093, subdivision 6, of the Penal Code.

Fourth. Did the trial court err in refusing to give defendant's proposed instruction No. 5?

No. That instruction read: 'You are instructed that in order to find the defendant guilty of murder in the first degree as a killing committed in the perpetration or attempted perpetration of robbery, you must find either:

'(1) That the defendant's purpose in seizing the rifle which is the People's Exhibit No. 34 in evidence was to effect a felonious taking as contained in the definition of robbery previously read to you, or

'(2) That the defendant's intention at or before the slaying was the felonious taking of property other than or in addition to People's Exhibit No. 34 in evidence.'

Defendant contends that since his requested instruction was not given, he was not permitted to have the jury properly informed as to what particular finding of facts from the evidence would have to be made in order to constitute the homicide mandatory first degree.

An examination of the instructions given reveals that defendant could not have suffered prejudice by reason of the omission of his requested instruction No. 5, because the instructions given amply covered the legal principles pertinent to the case.

Defendant's proposed instruction No. 5 merely elaborated upon the general instruction concerning section 189 of the Penal Code by dealing specifically with a killing committed in the perpetration, or attempted perpetration, or robbery, and by stating the elements necessary to a finding of robbery or attempted robbery.

The court gave a full and proper instruction covering section 189 of the Penal Code and, in addition, gave full and clear instructions covering the crime of robbery. Those instructions fully and properly informed the jury as to the findings necessary to reach a mandatory first-degree murder verdict.

Although defendant's requested instruction may have been a correct statement of the law, the law requires only that the trial court correctly instruct on any points of law pertinent to the issue. (Pen. Code, s 1093, subd. 6.) When the jury is properly instructed as to pertinent legal principles, the court need not restate those principles merely in another way. (People v. Chapman, supra, 207 Cal.App.2d 557, 579—580, 24 Cal.Rptr. 568.)

Fifth. Did the trial court commit prejudicial error on the penalty phase of the trial by instructing the jury 'in effect' that they were not to be influenced by pity or sympathy?

No. A court may not properly instruct a jury in the penalty phase of the trial that it cannot be influenced by pity for the defendant or sympathy for him. (People v. Polk, 63 A.C. 461, 469(13), 47 Cal.Rptr. 1, 406 P.2d 641.) However, in the present case the court did not, either in fact or in effect, so instruct the jury at the conclusion of the trial on the issue of penalty.

The court did instruct the jury prior to its deliberation on the guilt phase of the trial: 'Therefore, In determining the guilt or innocence of the defendant, you are to be governed solely by the evidence introduced in this trial and the law as stated to you by the Court.

'For such purpose, the law forbids you to be governed by mere sentiment, conjecture, sympathy, passion, prejudice, public opinion or public feeling.' (Italics added.) This instruction was appropriate on the issue of guilt. (People v. Polk, supra, at p. 469(13), 47 Cal.Rptr. 1, 406 P.2d 641.)

Two days after the jury had heard all the instructions relative to the guilt phase, the court instructed relative to the penalty phase, commencing the instructions: 'In the first phase of the trial, you were given general instructions concerning the standard by which the credibility of the witnesses was to be weighed, including that of expert witnesses. It will not be necessary to repeat at this time the general instructions with those others previously given to you.

'You are reminded that you are to be guided by the previous instructions given in the first phase of this case that are applicable to this phase of this case.'

Defendant argues that the jury was thus admonished to be guided by instructions given in the earlier guilt phase of the trial, necessarily including the instruction given relative to pity and sympathy. This contention is without merit.

The instruction given in the guilt phase was clearly limited to the jury's determination of the guilt or innocence of defendant.

The instruction given in the penalty phase made reference Solely to those guilt phase instructions, which were applicable to the penalty phase of the case. The jury could not reasonably have understood the inappropriate guilt phase instruction to be applicable to their deliberations on penalty.

A reading of the portion of instructions given in the penalty phase and quoted above makes clear that the jury could have understood only that the court was referring to those earlier instructions dealing with the credibility of witnesses and the weight and value of evidence.

The court made it absolutely clear that the question of penalty was committed entirely to the judgment and conscience of the jurors based upon their sound and absolute discretion. (See People v. Friend, 47 Cal.2d 749, 767, 306 P.2d 463.) The court placed no restrictions upon the exercise of the jury's judgment in the matter.

The judgment is affirmed.

McCOMB, Justice.

TRAYNOR, C.J., and PETERS, TOBRINER, PEEK, MOSK and BURKE, JJ., concur. Rehearing denied; PETERS, J., dissenting.

* * * * *

Robert Page Anderson joined 57 other condemned men at San Quentin, California, a prison opened in 1852 and located in an unincorporated town north of San Francisco in Marin County. Soon after his arrival, prison authorities on July 13, 1966 opened a second "death row." Usually, the prison had 18 men awaiting execution with nine or ten put to death in the gas chamber each year.

However, because high courts in California were giving criminals extra protection, nobody had been executed since January 23, 1963. With the number of men on death row pushing the facility beyond its designed capacity, Warden Lawrence W. Wilson took steps to enlarge the space from 60 to 90 cells.

The new portion of death row featured cells with more light than the other unit and the cells at eight by six feet were larger. Both rows of cells had the use of one television set for every three cells.

Anderson's daily routine was the same as other death row inmates. He was confined to his cell except for three and a half hours daily of exercise and conversation in a corridor. The corridor was only available for medical attention and occasional visits from relatives.

* * * * *

In a basement below Anderson's cell is the gas chamber, San Quentin's killing machine. It is next to a small holding cell where condemned men and women wait for possible last minute stays of execution. Whether or not Anderson took the time to learn the gas chamber's history and how it works is not known, but he would have heard plenty from other condemned men and perhaps the guards.

Condemned Row (more commonly referred to as Death Row) at San Quentin is divided into three sections: the quiet North-Segregation or North-Seg, built in 1934, for prisoners who "don't cause trouble"; the East Block, a crumbling, leaky maze of a place built in 1927; and the Adjustment Center for the "worst of the worst." Most of the prison's death row inmates resided in the East Block when Anderson was there.

The gas chamber was installed in San Quentin's basement in 1938. It is an eight-sided metal box, 6 feet across and 8 feet high and painted pale green. There is a 30-foot high chimney that goes outside to take the gas away. The chamber entrance is through a large rubber sealed door that looks more like a ship's hatch. A large locking wheel with five handles closes the door. There are large windows in five of the sides for witnesses to view the execution.

Inside the chamber are two identical metal chairs with perforated seats, marked "A" and "B." Two guards strap the prisoner into the chair, attaching straps across his upper and lower legs, arms, thighs and chest. They affix a Bowles stethoscope to the person's chest so that a doctor on the outside can monitor the heartbeat and pronounce death. Beneath the chair is a bowl filled with sulphuric acid mixed with distilled water to give a concentration of approximately 37%, with a pound of sodium cyanide pellets suspended in a gauze bag just above. After the door is sealed, and when the warden gives the signal, the executioner in a separate room operates a lever that releases the cyanide into the liquid. This causes a chemical reaction that releases hydrogen cyanide gas, which rises through the holes in the chair. ($2 NaCn + H_2SO_4 = 2 HCN + Na_2SO4$). When the reaction has finished the gas reaches a concentration of around 7,500 ppm.

The chemical reaction generates fumes of lethal hydrogen cyanide. The prisoner's eyes pop, the skin turns purple and the victim begins to drool. Then come spasms, as in an epileptic seizure. Because of the straps, however, involuntary body movements are restrained. Seconds after the prisoner first inhales, they will be unable to breathe, but will not lose consciousness immediately. Pain begins immediately and is felt in the arms, shoulders, back, and chest. The sensation is similar to the pain felt by a person during a heart attack, where essentially the heart is being deprived of oxygen.

As a result, the inmate dies of hypoxia, a form of oxygen starvation to the brain.

A study of 113 prisoners executed at San Quentin showed that the average time taken to kill them was 9.3 minutes. The prisoner will usually lose consciousness between one and three minutes after the gas hits their face and the doctor will pronounce them dead in around 10 to 12 minutes.

An exhaust fan then sucks the gas out of the chamber. Next, the corpse is sprayed with ammonia, which neutralises traces of the cyanide that may remain. After about half an hour, prison staff members enter the chamber, wearing gas masks and rubber gloves. Their training manual advises them to ruffle the victim's hair to release any trapped cyanide gas before removing the body.

Up until July 1966, 194 persons, including four women had been executed. The staff at San Quentin and condemned men on death row referred to the gas chamber as the "coughing box."

* * * * *

For the next two years, Robert Page Anderson saw the arrival of 26 more convicts sentenced to death bringing San Quentin's death row population to 84 men and one woman, the largest in history. He was also there when 37-year-old Aaron Mitchell took his last breath in the gas chamber on April 12, 1967.

Mitchell was convicted of murdering police officer Arnold Gamble in Sacramento during a shootout following a bar robbery on February 15, 1963. It would be the first and only execution during Ronald Reagan's term in office as California's governor.

* * * * *

Anderson did not know it at the time but he would never see anyone else led to the gas chamber. Like others on death row, he spent day after day, waiting for appeals to work their way through the judicial system. While the races, backgrounds and psychological make-up of those on death row differed, every convict locked in their cells had one thing in common; there was plenty of time to think about what happened and how it was that they ended up there wondering when they would die.

But then on November 18, 1968, Anderson learned that he might escape the gas chamber. He was going to get a new penalty trial. When he first got the news, he probably thought nothing had changed. On that day the California State Supreme Court upheld the state's death penalty, ruling on a 4-3 vote that capital punishment is not cruel and unusual and ruled that the two-trial system in capital cases, one to determine guilt and one to fix the penalty is constitutional. However, for Robert Anderson, he and another man Frederick Satterfield would get new penalty trials because persons opposed to capital punishment were excluded from their juries.

Satterfield was a 49-year-old carpenter who killed his common law wife, 30-year-old Patricia Satterfield and her 16-year-old daughter, Mary Alice Washington in their Santa Ana home on November 26, 1965. A telephone operator had traced a call for help. Mrs. Satterfield's daughter was in a bedroom, apparently phoning for help when she was shot.

Frederick Satterfield, a runner in the 1936 Junior Olympics had been angry because his common law wife was going to return to her husband. Patricia Satterfield, active in the National Association for Colored People (NAACP) and her daughter, an honor student, were shot in the head.

Frederick Satterfield had a history of violence. In 1950 he was convicted of killing Perry Lugrand, 44, a potential witness against him in a child-related offense.

An attorney who was a professor at Stanford University's Law School and associated with the NAACP's Legal Defense Fund championed Robert Anderson's case. The lawyer's name was Anthony Amsterdam who argued against capital punishment on four points: That juries were stacked with persons who have no objections to the death penalty. That juries are not instructed on factors to consider in setting penalties; that the death penalty is cruel and unusual punishment in today's society and that the law does not provide for court-appointed attorneys after trial and the first appeal.

Anderson now had a chance to avoid a trip to the coughing box.

The court ruled that prospective jurors in his first trial were "automatically excluded" when they said they were against the death penalty. Further problems were cited that the excused jurors in his first trial "did not make it unmistakenly clear that they would automatically vote against imposition of capital punishment without regard to any evidence or that their attitude would prevent them from making an impartial decision."

At this point, attorney Anthony Amsterdam left the case, and Anderson was assigned a public defender. On April 2, 1969, nearly four years to the day after the Hub Loans & Jewelry Company shootout, the second penalty trial for Anderson began in Department 12 of San Diego's Superior Court presided over by Judge Robert W. Conyers, a veteran of 20 years on the bench.

Judge Robert W. Conyers
(Courtesy San Diego County Judicial Services)

He declared that jury selection would be so thorough it would prevent automatic exclusion.

On the opening day of proceedings after a motion by Assistant Deputy District Attorney Robert Thomas, four prospective jurors, all married women were excused after they said they could not vote to impose the death penalty for any crime or under any circumstances.

One of the prospective jurors stated, "I oppose capital punishment. I have held this conviction for several years. Yes, I would vote against the death penalty under any circumstances. It is a barbarous custom."

The four women who were excluded had been questioned by defense attorney Robert Baxley and asked if they could impose the death penalty on a hired killer or the brutal murderer of a small child. All agreed they could not.

"I'm here to save this boy's life," Baxley had said during the questioning.

The second trial lasted 13 1/2 days but on April 23, 1969, the penalty verdict for Robert Page Anderson was the same as his first trial. The jury ruled in favor of once again imposing the death penalty on Anderson. A motion for a new trial was denied. The long process of appeal through the higher courts began for a second time and Anderson was sent to death row at San Quentin joining 101 others awaiting execution.

Chapter 13
The 1972 Ruling and Ramifications

In the fall of 1971 the California Supreme Court agreed to hear Robert Page Anderson's second appeal. However, on the eve of the Supreme Court hearing, his public defender suddenly died, leaving him without counsel. A young lawyer, Jerome B. Falk, fresh from a clerkship with U.S. Supreme Court Justice William O. Douglas, took Anderson's case for the appellate experience.

Along with Neri Ramos and attorneys with the American Civil Liberties Union, Falk stepped in to give Anderson his final chance to escape the gas chamber. Falk argued that capital punishment violated the state's constitution prohibiting "cruel and unusual punishment."

On February 18, 1972, the court in a six-to-one vote issued its decision. Anderson and his attorneys had won.

Chief Justice Donald R. Wright wrote the majority opinion and the *San Diego Union's* front page on February 19 had a photograph of the seven justices and above that was the headline **State Supreme Court Bans Death Penalty**. Under that was smaller font that read Life Terms Ordered for 107.

The story reported that the California Supreme Court ruled in *California v. Anderson* declaring that capital punishment is impermissible cruel and unusual punishment as it degraded and dehumanized the parties involved. It held that the penalty is "unnecessary to any legitimate goal of the state and is incompatible with the dignity of man and the judicial process".

Furthermore, the court also cited the view of capital punishment in American society as one of the most important reasons for its acceptability, contending that a growing population and decreasing amount of executions was persuasive evidence that such a punishment was no longer condoned by the general public.

The case also turned on a difference in wording between the U.S. Constitution's 8th Amendment argument against cruel and unusual and Article 1, Section 6 of the California Constitution, which read:

All persons shall be bailable by sufficient sureties, unless for capital offenses when the proof is evident or the presumption great. Excessive bail shall not be required, nor excessive fines imposed; nor shall cruel or unusual punishments be inflicted. Witnesses shall not be unreasonably detained, nor confined in any room where criminals are actually imprisoned.

Since the State Constitution prohibits a punishment, which is either of the two conditions (as opposed to prohibiting ones that violate both conditions), the court found the penalty unconstitutional on state constitutional grounds since if it violated either provision it was unconstitutional at the state level. Additionally, the court went so far as to decline to consider if the death penalty violates the Eighth Amendment to the United States Constitution since it had already found it to be in violation of the state constitution.

The state contended that while the use of capital punishment served no rehabilitating purposes, it was a legitimate punishment for retribution in serious offenses, in that it served to isolate the offender, and was a useful deterrent to crime. The court rejected the state's defense, citing that there were far less onerous means of isolating the offender, and the lack of proof that capital punishment is an effective deterrent.

Justice Marshall F. McComb was the lone dissenter.

Justice Marshall F. McComb
(Courtesy California Supreme Court Historical Society)

He argued that the death penalty deterred crime, noting numerous Supreme precedents upholding the death penalty's constitutionality (including 11 in the prior three and a half years), and stating that the legislative and initiative (ballot box) processes were the only appropriate avenues to determine whether the death penalty should be allowed.

* * * * *

Robert Page Anderson, an insignificant person all his life, now had achieved notoriety, not so much for whom he was but whom else would be impacted by the court's decision that caused all capital sentences in California to be commuted to life in prison with the possibility of parole. The ruling meant that any person ever charged with a murder committed in California before 1972 could not receive the death penalty.

Anderson and 101 other condemned men and five women would not be put to death. At the top of the high profile list was fellow death row inmate Charles Manson and four of his followers who had been sentenced to die for the Tate-LaBianca murders in 1969.

Also escaping lethal gas was Sirhan Sirhan who was awaiting execution for the assassination of Robert Kennedy.

At San Quentin, Associate Warden James W. Park, in the *San Diego Union* was quoted as saying, "most of the men are pretty happy" about the ruling. "There are no demonstrations or anything like that. Most of them are in a wait-and-see attitude."

In addition to Robert Anderson, three other San Diego men were included in the reprieve: Joseph Bernard Morse who in 1962 was 17, used a baseball bat and rock to club his mother and 12-year-old crippled sister to death in their Chula Vista home. Then in 1964 while awaiting trial, he strangled to death fellow jail inmate Thomas Taddei during an argument over a gambling debt.

The second condemned San Diego man to escape the gas chamber was Nathan Elmont Eli. On February 20, 1965, when he was 20, Eli murdered 24-year-old Constance Dunn, the wife of a Navy lieutenant and mother of two children. The murder was in her San Diego home while her husband was overseas. The victim was stabbed, raped and strangled to death while Eli was in her home to demonstrate a vacuum cleaner.

The other murderer whose death sentence was overturned was John David Hayes. Along with Anderson, all four were moved out of Death Row and returned to San Quentin's general population.

* * * * *

There was an immediate outcry from advocates of law and order who believed they had been betrayed by the judicial system and feared the release of many violent criminals. Heading the list of those voices was Governor Ronald Reagan. The governor, a staunch death penalty supporter had appointed Donald Wright as chief justice.

Chief Justice Donald Wright
(Courtesy California Supreme Court Historical Society)

Wright came to the court with a reputation of being a bright judge and excellent administrator, one who had two decades of experience as a Los Angeles Superior Court judge and Court of Appeal justice.

He also was a lifelong Republican, appointed by a conservative governor. So veteran justices assumed he would be conservative. But they quickly realized that Wright, unknown to the governor, adamantly opposed capital punishment and would write for the majority that banned the death penalty.

Governor Reagan bristled and said the court had placed itself "above the will of the people." He added that the decision made "a mockery of the constitutional processes involved in establishing the laws of California," and reinforced "the widespread concern of our people that some member of the judiciary inject their own philosophy into their decision rather than carry out their constitutional duty to interpret and enforce the law."

Law-and-order groups mobilized and in a few months had no difficulty collecting more than one million signatures on petitions to qualify Proposition 17 for the November ballot

In one of the most overwhelming public statements on record, Californians approved Proposition 17 with 67.5% voting Yes. On November 7, 1972, less than nine months after Anderson v. California had struck down the death penalty, the citizens of the state had reversed an activist state court decision and enforced the popular will regarding capital punishment. Rather than switch to the federal "cruel and unusual" standard, the amendment, kept the "cruel or unusual" standard, but it followed it with a clause that expressly declared the death penalty to be neither cruel nor unusual.

Despite passage of Proposition 17, no executions were carried out in California for the next 13 years. That was because a U.S. Supreme Court decision temporarily halted capital punishment in the United States resulting in extensive litigation.

Executions resumed on April 21, 1992 when Robert Alton Harris was put to death in the San Quentin gas chamber for the 1978 murders of two teenage boys in the north San Diego neighborhood of Mira Mesa. Three years earlier, in 1975 Harris had been convicted of involuntary manslaughter in the beating death of his brother's roommate. He served three years and was paroled in June 1978.

On July 5, 1978, after being out of prison and on the streets for only a month, Harris, then 25 and his 18-year-old brother Daniel stole two guns and were in San Diego planning a bank robbery. They ran into John Mayeski and Michael Baker, both 16, sitting in a green Ford LTD eating hamburgers in a supermarket parking lot. The boys wanted to spend the day fishing to celebrate Mayeski's newly acquired driver's license. Robert Harris commandeered

Mayeski's car and ordered him to drive to nearby Miramar Lake with his brother, Daniel following in another car. Harris told the boys they would be using their vehicle to rob a bank, but that no one would be hurt. At the lake, the Harris brothers ordered the boys to kneel. As they did they began to pray. Robert Harris told the boys to "Quit praying, and die like men." He then shot them multiple times.

The Harris brothers then returned to Robert's Mira Mesa home and finished the victims' half-eaten hamburgers while Robert bragged about the killings.

An hour later, the Harris brothers robbed a San Diego Trust and Savings Bank of $2,000. It was located across the street where they had kidnapped the two teenage boys. Less than an hour after the robbery, the Harris brothers were arrested. One of the officers who apprehended them was Steven Baker, father of murder victim Michael Baker, who at the time did not know that his son had been killed, let alone by one of the men he had just arrested.

* * * * *

After his conviction and several unsuccessful appeals and a last-second stay, Robert Alton Harris was executed in San Quentin's gas chamber on April 21, 1992, the first execution in California in 25 years. For his last meal, he asked for and was given a 21-piece bucket of Kentucky Fried Chicken, two large Domino's pizzas, a bag of jelly beans, a six-pack of Pepsi, and a pack of Camel cigarettes.

Harris's brother, Daniel was convicted of kidnapping and sentenced to six years in state prison. He was released in 1983.

Chapter 14
The Last Interview

Robert Page Anderson, after serving 11 years and four months, seven years of his sentence on death row, was paroled from San Quentin and released in December 1976. The minimum sentence for life in prison with the possibility of parole was seven years. The California Adult Authority on February 26, 1976 established automatic eligibility for parole for Anderson at 11 years and six months. He was placed on parole two months early so he could enroll in college in Seattle, Washington where he had family.

Earlier in 1975, Anderson enrolled in a literacy program and completed high school diploma requirements despite not having full use of both hands, the result of being wounded when he was captured.

San Diego Union reporter, Frank Stone, in a December 10, 1976 story quoted Harold Riddell, assistant to the chairman of the Adult Authority who said, "Anderson's long-term excellent adjustment and the length of time served (in San Quentin Prison) were the dominant factors in his release on parole." Riddell also said, "Anderson maintained an excellent attitude despite the loss of his hands. There were no psychiatric problems involving his release."

* * * * *

The last traces the author was able to find of Anderson were two stories written by *Los Angeles Times* reporter Richard A. Serrano in April 1990. The first, titled "I Wish I Never Got Off That Bus," gave Anderson's view of what happened on the day of the Hub Loans & Jewelry Company shootout.

"Robert Page Anderson rode the bus downtown, planning to trade a diamond ring at the Hub Jewelry & Loan Co. (SIC), a pawnshop at the corner of 5th Avenue and F Street in the Gaslamp Quarter.

It was 25 years ago this month. April 8, 1965.

Light rain fell outside as Anderson, a puny, self-described "22-year-old man going on 15" walked through the door. What happened inside, and the four hours of fierce gun battle that ensued, went down as the most dramatic police operation in San Diego history at that time. One man was killed, two others wounded. More than 1,000 rounds of ammunition were fired. A newspaperman at the scene suffered a heart attack and died. A man trapped in the two-story structure eventually lost his eyesight from the tear gas tossed by police through the bullet-shattered windows.

In the years ahead, Anderson would be sentenced to death, then win a celebrated reprieve when the state Supreme Court used his case to overturn the death penalty for every prisoner on Death Row in 1972. For San Diego police, the lessons learned that rainy day in April would translate into the creation of the first fully equipped SWAT unit, trained by then-Sgt. Allen D. Brown, the hero of the day who crept into the building and shot Anderson.

Anderson had planned to hock the diamond ring, but didn't like the way credit manager Louis Richards, 61, a white man, was acting toward him, a black man. Anderson had lived his life in the San Diego black community. He did not understand white people, he said in an interview last week with The Times, nor did he trust or like them.

Anderson, 53, sat for a seven-hour interview in his tiny apartment in a poor neighborhood in Seattle. At times, he paced about the room, reliving the murder, his eyes widening as he waved a steel curtain rod through the air, pretending it was the rifle he used to kill the pawnshop manager and shoot at police.

When Anderson didn't like the way he was being treated by Richards, he asked to see a .30-06 rifle. He asked for ammunition. He started to load as Richards bolted for the door. He swung to his left and fired; Richards fell dead on the floor with a hole in the back.

Anderson knelt over the dead man's body, his mind racing. "I didn't see any movement," he said. "I thought, 'God, this guy's dead.' And I got scared. I told myself I had to do something to protect myself. And there was no way I was going to walk out there and give myself up."

He smashed open the gun cases, snatching up bullets as police sirens grew louder outside. "I started loading all those suckers up," he said. Another clerk, 63-year-old Theodore Swienty, hid upstairs, sliding underneath a bed and praying that his feet weren't showing. Anderson never found him, but Swienty later suffered permanent eye injuries from the tear gas.

More than 60 officers surrounded the building. Nicknamed "Rabbit," Anderson sprinted up and down the stairs, firing about 80 rounds out the windows to keep police at bay. The police responded with about 800 shots of their own. A Navy gunner's mate tossed concussion grenades at the building. At one point, the police even threw soda bottles to break open the pawnshop windows, many of them still painted black from the old bomb-scare days during World War II.

"When the Coke bottles missed, the crowd actually booed," recalled Armond Viora, a key shop operator across the street who joined hundreds of other bystanders.

Police Sgt. Samuel R. Chasteen was injured in the forehead, either from an Anderson bullet or flying debris. Robert A. Crandall, a newspaper editor working for the San Diego Independent, was overcome at the scene when he suffered a heart attack and died.

The light rain kept falling. "I wanted to get away," Anderson said. "Don't you dig? I wasn't going to put nothing down or give anything up until I got away."

Four hours into the standoff, Sgt. Brown went inside. He found Anderson on the darkened mezzanine, a pistol in each hand.

Brown fired first, hitting Anderson at close range with buckshot from the .12-gauge pump-action shotgun, leaving a half-dollar-size hole in the wall embedded with Anderson's blood. The police sergeant fired a total of three times, blasting Anderson in both arms and the lower left side. Anderson spun and crumpled to the floor.

"I thought I had cut him in half," said Brown, now retired. "But when the light reflected on him, I was amazed that he was still breathing. He lay there on the floor and swore like you wouldn't believe. I thought, 'Here's a real animal, his stomach pumping blood out and swearing at us officers.'"

Anderson remembers it somewhat differently. He insists he would have dropped the pistols if only Brown had ordered him to. "I didn't want to kill him," he said of Brown. "I gave him his life."

Brown scoffs at the statement, saying that Anderson's guns clicked twice, and would have gone off had he not stuffed the chambers with mixed ammunition. "Why didn't he just throw his hands up?" Brown asked.

* * * * *

The second interview in 1990 by Richard Serrano was to get Anderson's opinion about Robert Alton Harris who then was on death row and would not be executed for another two years. The stories' headline was:
 A Killer Has No Pity for Harris: Reaction: Man who beat Death Row and whose appeal spared dozens of others says Harris deserves to die: 'He was way out of line.'

SEATTLE — Convicted murderer Robert Page Anderson, a survivor of three execution dates whose appeal overturned capital punishment in California and spared the lives of such notorious killers as Charles Manson and Sirhan Sirhan, holds no pity for Robert Alton Harris.

More than a decade apart, Anderson and Harris committed murder in San Diego. Both were sentenced to die. But while Harris sits today on Death Row at San Quentin prison awaiting the gas chamber, Anderson is a free man-- paroled after he appealed his sentence for shooting a pawnshop manager.

The 1972 appellate decision, which made Anderson briefly famous, overturned every death sentence in the state, canceling execution dates for more than 100 inmates then on Death Row.

Though Anderson lived, he thinks Harris should die.

"That was wrong, what he did," Anderson said in an interview with The Times last week in his $80-a-month Seattle apartment.

"He was way out of line. He could have let those kids go. So I have no pity or compassion for somebody like that. I can't, in good conscience, be in his corner. I can't. And if those kids' parents sit there in the front row and clap when he dies, I still couldn't sympathize with Robert Harris.

"I don't want him to live. I want him to die because he killed children."

The words came in a fast clip from the 53-year-old Anderson, his black hair now faded white and his cheeks encased in a full gray beard. His beliefs seem harsh and contradictory, coming from a man who once stood five days from an execution date.

Although Anderson is now a law-and-order advocate who favors gun control and supports capital punishment in cases involving children, he maintains that execution was wrong for him because he says he killed a man on the spur of the moment. He believes Harris, who killed two San Diego high school boys in 1978, should be executed because his victims were teen-agers.

Yet, for opponents of capital punishment, Robert Page Anderson today represents a living testimonial that there is some good worth saving in every man.

Released from prison in 1976, Anderson has adjusted to life outside without the use of his hands, which were crippled in his shoot-out with San Diego police 25 years ago. He has tutored preschool children at day-care centers and served as a counselor for juvenile delinquents.

In 1972, the state Supreme Court used Anderson's case to review the death penalty and then abolished that statute as cruel and unusual punishment. The Times wrote then that Anderson's "name like those of Gideon and Miranda now belongs to history."

Four years later, Anderson was released from prison and eventually completed his parole and slipped out of the state, moving to the Pacific Northwest to begin a new life. He tried to forget his past failures and hoped his name would never again be heard of by the people of California.

"I'm at peace now," he said. "God believes you can rehabilitate yourself, and that's what I'm all about.

"I remember the preacher on Death Row said that some crimes you have to pay for, but I kept saying I wanted to go home. I told the state that if they would let me out, I'd never commit a crime again. I told them, 'Just open up the prison door and kick me out.' "

There are plenty of people, especially in San Diego, who believe Anderson unfairly eluded the gas chamber, feelings they harbor to this day. Among them is Allen Brown, the San Diego police officer who shot Anderson 25 years ago. "He took another man's life," Brown said of Anderson. "He tried to take mine."

* * * * *

In 2018, James Biggins, Jr.'s 83-year-old widow, Jutta in a telephone interview from her Rancho Santa Fe home remembers her husband defending Robert Anderson.

James and Jutta Biggins
(Courtesy Jutta Biggins)

Two things stand out in her memory. The first is that she had never seen her husband at work so on the opening day of the trial, unbeknownst to her husband she hired a babysitter to watch their three children and went to the courthouse. Not wanting to make her husband nervous, she said she sat in the back row of seats, hunched down and hopefully out of sight.

That night when her husband came home he told her, "Funny, there was a black guy in the court seats with blonde hair. Maybe this case is getting to me."

It turns out Jutta Biggins with blonde hair was hiding behind the man and Biggins, seeing only her hair, thought the black man was a blonde.

At the time she did not tell him she was the one sitting in court but after the trial was over confessed to what happened.

Her husband's response, "You should have told me. I thought I was losing my mind."

Jutta Biggins other memory is something that did not happen often with convicted criminals her husband represented. She said he received a letter of appreciation from Anderson thanking Biggins for his work.

In the letter Anderson wrote, "I should have gone to the movie."

Robert Page Anderson died on August 3, 1999. He was 62.

(Courtesy San Diego History Center)

* * * * *

On July 16, 2014, in a unanimous decision, a three-judge panel of the United States Ninth Circuit Court of Appeals ruled that California's death penalty system was unconstitutional because it is arbitrary and plagued with delay.

Writing the opinion was Judge Cormac J. Carney. However, the decision was made on a technicality that the argument submitted by lawyers on both sides did not address the question of whether life on death row in California constituted cruel and unusual punishment only that it is unconstitutional.

As of July 2018 there were nearly 750 people on California's death row including 22 women. That was more than twice as many people as the next highest state—Florida with 347. California has executed 13 people since 1992 and none since 2006 when a federal court ruled that the State's lethal injection procedures violated the constitutional ban on cruel and unusual punishment.

Chapter 15
The Anti-Sniper Platoon and SWAT Unit

After the April 8, 1965 shootout at the Hub Loans &
Jewelry Company, it was apparent that the San Diego
Police Department had to be better prepared for the future.
Nothing on the scale of what happened that day had ever
been seen in the city before.

(Courtesy KGTV, KFMB-TV and San Diego Police
Museum)

(Courtesy KGTV, KFMB-TV and San Diego Police
Museum)

The Hub shootout escalated from one gunman holed up
in a building, to a standoff that paralyzed a large part of
downtown San Diego. Police leaders were nervous about
what was going on elsewhere in the nation including large,
violent civil rights disturbances and massive protests
against the Viet Nam War.

For San Diego, the need for an immediate, effective
response to the kind of incident that happened at the Hub
would not necessarily avert large-scale civil disobedience
seen elsewhere but it was thought that having a trained
unit to arrive quickly on the scene was a way to take out a
sniper or accomplices before things got out of hand. After
what police went through at the Hub, they wanted to make
sure the city was not caught off guard like that again.

No one had a clear, complete idea how to plan, man,
activate and supervise a specialized police unit, but
everyone knew if anyone could do it, it was Sergeant
Allen D. Brown, the hero of the Hub Loans & Jewelry

Company shootout.

(Courtesy KGTV, KFMB-TV and San Diego Police
Museum)

Enthusiasm was high but three years passed before the
team would be close to completion. During those years,
police leadership anxiously watched what was going on
elsewhere and joined city leaders in hoping the same
would not happen in San Diego. On August 11, 1965,
rioting, looting and arson broke out in the Los Angeles
suburb of Watts. Five days later, 34 people had been killed,
more than a thousand were injured and some 3,500
arrested. Damage was estimated at $40 million.

* * * * *

After he was asked to set up a separate police unit, Sergeant Brown, with the help of others began forming a plan. The name for the unit that Brown liked was the Anti-Sniper Platoon (ASP) because the acronym brought to mind the poisonous snake.

Dave Hall was an original member of the ASP unit.

Dave Hall 1968 and 2018

At 76, in a 2018 interview at his San Diego home, Hall said the name ASP was also picked for an identity reason.

"We did not want to be known as SWAT and associated with the Los Angeles Police Department," he said. "The LAPD was one of the first in the U.S. to have what it called a Special Weapons and Tactics (SWAT) team."

The first snipers to be considered were patrol officers with military experience and it was important that they had their own rifles. But two years after Brown was told to form his team, it was still not ready. In the 1967 photo below, taken at USMC Base, Camp Pendleton, Brown demonstrates sniper techniques to new officers.

(Courtesy Brown family)

By then, Allen D. Brown had been promoted from sergeant to lieutenant and while he was making it known the names of officers he wanted to serve under him on the ASP unit, more than three years would pass since the Hub shootout and the team was still not in place.

* * * * *

A key person Lieutenant Brown turned to for help in organizing and equipping the ASP team was Sergeant Terry Truitt. Truitt specialized in planning and training. In a 1966 photo below, he is shown instructing officers on how to identify outlaw motorcycle gangs and was considered an expert in the Western United States.

(Courtesy Terry Truitt)

In 2018, Truitt, 82, shared memories at his Escondido home of the Anti-Sniper Platoon's early years and what he was asked by Lieutenant Brown.

Terry and Sandy Truitt

"When he told me he was going to put a team together," Truitt said, "He asked me, 'Who do you want?' I told him we needed men who had been around a long time so we could rely on them. I knew we needed guys who were not going to fly off half-cocked."

Truitt said a few members of the police brass were leery about some of the men recommended. "They looked at us as rebels," Truitt said with a chuckle. "Not long after the list came out, some were transferred to investigations."

* * * * *

Moving forward, A.D. Brown wrote two memos on May 7, 1968 to Assistant Police Chief Edwin "E.C" DeBolt and Captain Michael Sgobba.

Edwin "E.C." DeBolt

Michael Sgobba
(Courtesy San Diego Police Museum and The Informant)

In the first memo, Brown lists the officers who wanted to join the ASP team.

```
7 May 1968

Chief DeBolt

Capt. MA Sgobba

Anti-Sniper squads
_____

   The following individuals have expressed an interest in the
squad:

   TRUITT, Terry          Sgt *
   BECKER, Edward         Pat
   DURHAM, Earl           Pat *
   GLEASON, Gary          Pat
   GRIFFIN, Larry         Pat
   HALL, Dave             Pat
   HENRY, Dale            Pat *
   LADD, Ronald           Pat
   McDANIEL, Robert       Pat
   McMANUS, Robert        Pat
   SCHMIDT, John          Pat
   SHIVELY, James         Pat
   SIMMS, Wayne           Pat
   SKRAK, Richard         Pat *
   SPURLOCK, Gene         Pat *
   VANDIVER, Hugh         Pat
   WALLS, David           Pat

   * indicates that the man owns a .30-06 rifle
```

The second memo lists the men Brown considered the best of the best.

CITY of SAN DIEGO

MEMORANDUM

7 May 1968

Capt. MA Sgobba

Sgt. TJ Truitt

Anti-Sniper Squad

The memo from Chief DeBolt requires that you select an anti-sniper squad from the
17 men listed on the attached memo. I feel that the following men have the attributes necessary to make up a good sniper team:

DURHAM, Earl
GLEASON, Gary
GRIFFIN, Larry
HENRY, Dale
SHIVELY, James

GLEASON should be on the team because he is going to be instrumental in the training
of the teams. His vast experience along these lines in Viet Nam make him an invaluable man in an anti-sniper team. The other men have demonstrated, to me at least, the necessary field experience and are cool under trying circumstances.

Gary Gleason, 74, in a 2018 telephone interview from his Chula Vista home told of his three tours of duty in Viet Nam as a Navy SEAL.

Gary Gleason April 1967 and 2015
(Courtesy Gary Gleason and Bob Lampert)

After coming home, Gleason graduated from the San
Diego Police Department's Academy in July1967.

Gary Gleason July 1967 and (far right) 1997 Narcotics
Division
(Courtesy Gary Gleason)

When Gleason left the Navy as an E-4 Third Class
Petty Officer, he still had reserve commitments and feared
the Navy might recall him to active duty so he joined the
Army National Guard in San Diego to remain with the
police department. He then became the primary training
officer for Lieutenant Brown's anti-sniper team.

"We worked with the military," he said, "to get arms
and training with high-powered weapons." But Gleason
said the Army was not the most cooperative in supplying
the fledging unit enough resources for what they needed.

Gleason eventually became a lieutenant colonel in the
Guard and after serving 15 years with the police
department, rising to the rank of homicide detective he
joined the San Diego County District Attorney for 22
years and became commander of investigations before
retiring in 2005.

"Lieutenant Brown did a great job putting the anti-sniper team together," he said. But it was a long time before it was fully in place.

* * * * *

Gleason's connection to the Army National Guard and his ability to scrounge for things enabled the unit to use an Army truck to help with training at Camp Elliott, an abandoned Marine Corps base just east of present Marine Corps Air Station, Miramar.

Gary Gleason (left)
(Courtesy Terry Truitt)

At Camp Elliott, ASP members practiced rappelling off the sides of buildings (Truitt and Hall shown) and practicing high-risk raids and invasions.

(Courtesy Terry Truitt)

Brown and his ASP team foraged for everything they could get. As Dave Hall said, "Even with what happened at the Hub shootout, it was hard to convince the powers-to-be that a special unit was needed."

Terry Truitt chuckled when he remembered Captain
Michael Sgobba asking him to put together a plan on how
to handle a large-scale riot in Southeast San Diego.

Michael Sgobba
(Courtesy S.D.P.O.A.)

"He told me he wanted a one-page brief," Truitt said
with a smile. When Truitt returned with details how to
cope with such a major event, Sgobba recoiled in horror as
Truitt handed him a two-inch thick report. "In a loud voice
he said, 'I don't have time to look at all this.'"

* * * * *

In a June 25, 1968 memorandum from Brown to
Inspector W.F. Garlington, Brown wrote that he hoped that
Garlington and other members of the administration would
accept ASP as the unit's official name. He outlined some
of the team's needs:

"Rifle Box: As you know our four 30.06 rifles have been
carefully 'zeroed in' and it is possible to knock the sights
out of adjustment while transporting them with other

equipment to a staging area. I therefore request the construction of a wooden box to contain and protect the rifles during transportation.

"Coveralls: Officers risk damaging and soiling their uniforms during canyon searches; taking injured persons out of automobiles that have been in an accident, particularly from an automobile that has left the road and gone into a brushy area; in building and neighborhood searches, over fences and onto the roofs of buildings for criminal suspects. In the event of a prolonged riot, officers could don coveralls and protect their uniforms. The ASP officers will be asked to go into action under very dangerous conditions during which they may have to 'hit the dirt,' crawl, and move in areas that would ruin a uniform. An officer reluctant to get his uniform dirty may be seriously injured by gunfire.

"Sears sells coveralls at two prices--$6.00 and $10.00 with a reduced prices in lots of 50 or more pairs. Included with this report are four pairs of coveralls for evaluation. They may be long or short-sleeved; they have a two-way zipper, that is the zipper may be opened from the bottom or top. I suggest the long-sleeved coveralls to protect the officer's arms or if worn over his uniform, it will protect his shirtsleeves. The $10.00 overall has a perm-press, both overalls may be washed and ironed.

"Web Belts and other gear: The ASP officers should be furnished with web belts to which may be attached a canvas web holster for the officers .38, two canvas pouches, one pouch can easily carry two tear gas grenades, the other pouch may carry shotgun or rifle ammunition. I recommend at least 18 belts (88¢ to 98¢ each) 36 pouches (69¢ each) and 18 holsters (98¢ each). Total outlay would be about $50.00.

Tear Gas Box: I further request the construction of a wooden box to contain at least 12 tear gas grenades, the type that may be thrown into a building without fear of fire. This will avoid confusion as to what type of grenade should be sent to the ASP group during an emergency. A cardboard box may be used to transport web gear to the staging area.
"If approved, the sizes of the boxes will be worked out a later date."

* * * * *

One of the earliest records of Lieutenant Brown's anti-sniper platoon were photos and the names of 18 officers who were on three teams in 1968. They are shown wearing the Sears overalls that Larry Truitt recommended to Lieutenant Brown.

Left to right Team 1: Sergeant Larry Shanley
Officers Ron Collins, Gary Morris, Gerry Bobb, Gene Dillon, Tom Piell.

Left to right Team 2: Sergeant Larry Gore
Officers Sandy Strong, Roer Michaels, Bill Kreder,
Herbert J. Hulet, Scott Naliboff

Left to right Team 3: Sergeant Terry Truitt
Officers Dave Hall, Gary Gleason, Dick Skrak, Earl
Durham, D.K. Henry
  (Courtesy San Diego Police Museum and Terry Truitt)

   While logistics and how to pay for Brown's unit were
still being worked out, a major test for San Diego police
came in the summer of 1969 when law enforcement,

including the Federal Bureau of Investigation (FBI) was
trying to disrupt and neutralize local chapters of the Black
Panther Party (BPP) and US, another black power group.
Tensions had been building since May 23, 1969 after BPP
member John Savage was killed by rival members of US.
On June 16, 1969, the San Diego Police Department raided
the Black Panther's office at 2608 Imperial Avenue, one of
two headquarters on that street (the other was at 2952 1/2
Imperial Avenue).

In July 1969, on the eve of the Apollo 11 mission to the
moon, an altercation between San Diego police and a
black youth led to days of racial unrest. The flash point
was at Mountain View Park, a seven block narrow stretch
of green two blocks south of Imperial Avenue along the
east side of 40th Street. The park, bisected by busy Ocean
View Boulevard was a popular gathering place for the
community with picnic tables, basketball courts, sport's
fields and a nearby community center. It also is two blocks
south of Greenwood Memorial Park Cemetery, where Hub
manager Louis Richards is buried.

The confrontation, late on a warm Sunday afternoon
July 13, 1969 saw the presence of lines of police officers
on a ridge overlooking the park. Many were outfitted with
gas masks.

(Courtesy KGTV, KFMB-TV and San Diego Police Museum)

(Courtesy KGTV, KFMB-TV and San Diego Police Museum)

Later it was reported that police Inspector William
Gore said violence broke out when police stopped to cite a
motorist who had refused to move his car parked illegally
at 40th Street and Franklin Avenue at the far north end of
Mountain View Park.

Inspector William Gore
(Courtesy San Diego Police Museum)

A crowd from the park surrounded the officers who
called for assistance by radio. As police moved into the
park in numbers, gunfire from snipers began.

A 19-year-old man, Bruce Lewis opened fire on police
at close range with a semi-automatic rifle. Police returned
fire and killed him.

It was then that 17-year-old Robert White grabbed
Lewis's rifle and began firing at officers. It also was the
moment when KOGO-TV photographer Bob Lampert who
was on the scene filming the breaking news story for
Channel 10, put down his camera and shifted into his role
as a San Diego Reserve Police Officer.

Lampert recalled what happened:

Bob Lampert
(Courtesy Bob Lampert)

"I was there at the very beginning and a suspect from the park (Bobby White) was shooting at officers above on the hill (west of the park) when Chief Roed showed up. White continued shooting and sent rounds over Chief Roed's head.

Police Chief Olif J. "O.H." Roed
(Courtesy San Diego Police Museum)

"I was working as a photographer for Channel 10 at the time but was also a (Police) Reserve. I was filming across towards where the shooting was coming from and was also a member of the Police Revolver Club and shot sometimes with Team 2.

(Courtesy KGTV, KFMB-TV and San Diego Police Museum)

"I could tell that the officers shooting weren't hitting the mark so I put down my camera, borrowed an officers revolver and fired two rounds knocking the suspect (White) to the ground. I then picked up my camera and filmed the arrest."

* * * * *

Bob Lampert was honored with a Golden Mic award for the video he shot on that day but the shots he fired from a service revolver were kept secret until years later.

The shooting investigation was conducted by Homicide and because of Lampert's positions as a TV news photographer and a Reserve officer; the incident was handled as a "Special Investigation" and never publicized.

Bob Lampert with Homicide Lieutenant Ed Stevens
1970's
(Courtesy Bob Lampert)

    Shooting victim Robert White was taken to County
Hospital where he was treated for a wound described as
not serious and then placed in Juvenile Hall. The shootings
though, sparked a riot that included a rash of arson fires,
several burglaries and two robberies by roving gang
members.

(Courtesy KGTV, KFMB-TV and San Diego Police
Museum)

    Inspector Gore said he had evidence that some of those
who later rioted were monitoring police radio calls and
relaying formation to bands of followers via CB radio.
    A gasoline bomb nearly destroyed the Farmers Market
at Euclid and Logan Avenues.

Deputy Police Chief W.J. Morrison said two anonymous telephone calls warned of plans to storm the downtown police headquarters and patrolling officers encountered several caravans of agitators on city streets headed toward the station.

Just before 10 P.M., officers were able to intervene and break them up while twelve officers with a municipal court warrant raided Black Panther headquarters at 2952 ½ Imperial Avenue.

(Courtesy KGTV, KFMB-TV and San Diego Police Museum)

Inspector Ray Hoobler, who would become police chief in 1971, led the raid. After breaking down the office door, officers found no one inside.

Ray Hoobler
(Courtesy KGTV, KFMB-TV and San Diego Police
Museum)

What they discovered were two rifles, a shotgun, gas
masks and a clock on the wall with a clear message.

(Courtesy KGTV, KFMB-TV and San Diego Police
Museum)

   Near the Panther's office, police arrested three men in a
car after finding a shotgun hidden under the hood and a
pistol concealed in the passenger glove compartment.

(Courtesy KGTV, KFMB-TV and San Diego Police
Museum)
   When it was over, two people had been killed, at least
six injured and nearly a hundred people arrested on a
variety of charges. Upwards of 25 stores were damaged by
fire or looters. As a precaution, police began working 12-
hour shifts with no days off for ten days.
                            * * * * *

    Helping ease simmering tensions below the surface in the neighborhoods around Mountain View Park was something that happened exactly one week later. On a Sunday night, the eyes of the entire world were on a surface 238,900 miles away when astronaut Neil Armstrong took his "one small step for man, one giant leap for mankind" on the moon.

* * * * *

    Four-and-a-half years after the Hub Loans & Jewelry Company shootout and three months following the Black Panther incident in the Mountain View area, Lieutenant Brown's newly formed team had not been involved in a major incident. But it was in place and on call as seen in an October 21, 1969 roster list from Brown.

    Three 12-man teams plus Allen Brown were on call and as the memo that follows shows; Brown's preferred name (ASP) for the unit was still in place. While Gary Gleason, the patrolman with Viet Nam experience who was Brown's top choice for the unit was not shown on the list; Gleason says he was on Team III.

```
                SPECIAL WEAPONS TEAMS
              ANTI-SNIPER PLATOON (ASP)

          LT. A. D. BROWN, COMMANDING OFFICER
                  TELEPHONE 583 7358


  TEAM I
     Sgt. R. J. Thorburn            274 2468
          R. E. Collins            298 9493
          F. L. Kenney             447 0332 (Poway)
          F. W. McCann             281 2007
         *R. S. Michelson          283 4876
          G. W. Morris             469 1308
          T. M. Piell              277 0385
         *E. J. Sergott            447 2874
          L. D. Triplett           447 0930
         *J. S. Varley             222 9174
          R. B. Wallis             423 3367
          J. H. Warden             435 2363 (Coronado)


  TEAM II
     Sgt. J. V. Mullen             295 1132
          G. R. Brown              278 2845
         *C. M. Hale               582 5815
          R. E. Hannibal           460 6088
          R. B. Michael            276 6332
          T. B. Morse              264 1986
         *W. L. Moser              277 9444
          S. D. Naliboff           277 7783
          R. G. Newman             420 6929
          A. F. Quick              460 3056
         *C. A. Redding            279 1518
          S. A. Strong             282 0222


  TEAM III
     Sgt. T. J. Truitt             278 5296
          M. C. Alber              448 7119
          W. R. Ashcraft           281 4548
         *W. Bird                  278 6391
          E. T. Durham             583 8034
         *J. T. Heacock            460 2366
          R. E. McManus            442 6400
          D. C. Sanford            479 6489
          R. Skrak                 465 9240
         *J. C. Swallow            274 8472
          G. E. Thomas             488 3996
          D. Worden                278 7816

  NOTE: Call Lt. Brown at any time there is sniper
        activity and a sniper team is called.

  * Indicates Northern Division personnel.

  PART II APPENDIX VIII-A

  October 21, 1969
```

(Courtesy San Diego Police Museum)

Another person not listed on the memo was Larry Gore who was a sergeant on the original ASP team and a member of Team 2.

Larry Gore
(Courtesy San Diego Police Museum)

Gore, 77, in a 2018 telephone interview from his San Diego home talked about the early challenges of the anti-sniper platoon.

"Just about everything was rudimentary. We were able to get some firearms from the military including MP5's." (The MP5 was a 9mm submachine gun, developed in the 1960's by Heckler & Koch, a German small arms manufacturer and became a weapon-of-choice for SWAT units.)

2018 photo of SWAT officer Dave Speck with MP5 at
police target range

Larry Gore was not on the scene of the Hub shootout but was part of another SWAT action in 1984 that is described later. In 1992 after retiring from the police department he went on to be the chief of police in West Sacramento, California until 1999.

Larry Gore
(Courtesy Bob Lampert)

He and his wife, Susie, reside in the San Diego neighborhood of Scripps Ranch.

* * * * *

At some point, after the special unit was selected, equipped, trained and put on stand-by, it was given a new name. The Anti-Sniper Platoon (ASP) became Special Weapons and Tactics (SWAT).

(Courtesy Terry Truitt)

Until 1970, equipment for uniformed officers sent to large-scale incidents and deployed in riot formations such as the one at Mountain View Park did not include face shields.

(Courtesy KGTV, KFMB-TV and San Diego Police Museum)

Richard Bennett, a San Diego Police officer from 1961-2001, writing for the San Diego Police Museum web page stated that the first time that face shields were used was 1970.

Richard Bennett
(Courtesy Steve Willard and San Diego Police Museum)

They were kept in the armory at headquarters and when riot formations were ordered, the face shields were brought to the scene from downtown.

Bennett wrote that it was during the Ocean Beach riots of 1970 that face shields were requested, but a field lieutenant decided not to wait and sent officers on foot to clear a vacant field at Nimitz and West Point Loma without face shields. The result was that Wilford J. ("Irish") O'Neal was struck in the face with a jagged chunk of concrete.

"Irish" O'Neal
(Courtesy Steve Willard)

O'Neal lost an eye, and never returned to work.

* * * * *

In August 1974, seven months after Lieutenant A.D. Brown had retired, the San Diego Police Department took a major step to serve and protect the public, while at the same time protecting themselves. The city council approved using $50,000 in federal monies to buy a bulletproof van for the police.

The van had a protective lining and was stocked with communications, weapons and other police equipment. The air-conditioned vehicle had its own lighting and public address system.

Then councilmember Maureen O'Connor, who would go on to be elected San Diego's mayor from 1986-1992, said the bulletproof police van caused her to worry about "overkill." She added, "Now we've got the guns and the tank." Police eyes rolled when she asked, "What happened to the bobbies?" referring to London policemen who carry only a nightstick and a whistle.

Assistant Police Chief Mike Sgobba assured the council that the specially equipped van would be utilized by the police tactical unit only in situations "where there is a very serious threat to life."

* * * * *

The Hub Loans and Jewelry Company shootout was the event that eventually led to the formation of a SWAT unit for the San Diego Police Department. And as the years passed, the team was called to respond to violent flash points. One of those came five years after A.D. Brown retired.

It was a Monday morning on January 29, 1979 in the east San Diego suburban neighborhood of San Carlos. Just as the bell rang to signal the start of classes at Grover Cleveland Elementary, a rifle crack was heard at around 8:30 A.M. Children waiting in front of the school began falling to the ground, bleeding. Gunfire continued.

Confused teachers, parents and students took awhile to realize that a sniper somewhere in houses across the street was picking off students. First to the side of fallen students was Cleveland elementary principal, Burton Wragg, The 53-year-old man who enjoyed weekend camping trips with his family was married and the father of two sons and a daughter. He tried to help the students and move them out of harm's way. But then came another gunshot and Wragg fell bleeding from a chest wound. Rushing to his side was the school custodian, 56-year-old school, Mike Suchar. He, too, was shot. Teachers and students barricaded themselves in the school, while nurses treated the wounded but four victims were still outside.

Minutes later when 30-year-old Robert Robb, the first
San Diego police officer arrived, he got a bullet in his neck.

Robert Robb
(Courtesy San Diego Police Museum)

The gunfire was coming from a house directly across
the street. Shots came from different windows, as it
seemed the sniper was trying to locate the best vantage
point. Helicopters hovered overhead and specially trained
officers telephoned the person in the house. The voice that
answered seemed to be that of a young, soft-spoken girl.
When officers tried to negotiate a surrender she hung up
several times, saying she was "having too much fun."

The shooting continued until another police officer and
a security guard from a neighboring high school,
commandeered a garbage truck and drove it in front of the
school, blocking the sniper's field of fire.

A newspaper reporter, after learning the address police
had pinpointed as the sniper's nest dialed the phone

number at the house. A young girl answered. She was
asked if she knew where the shots were coming from. She
gave her home address and when the reporter told her it
was her own address, she said, "Yeah, who do you think's
doing the shooting?"

The reporter asked her why?

"I don't like Mondays. This livens up the day," was her
answer.

The shooting lasted a half hour. After thirty-six shots
had been fired, a standoff between the girl and the San
Diego SWAT team lasted six hours. When it was over, the
girl, 16-year-old Brenda Spencer, a wisp of a girl with
stringy strawberry blonde hair and large glasses, emerged
out the front door. With helmeted and face-shielded
SWAT officers aiming sawed-off shotguns and high-
powered rifles at her, she laid down a .22 caliber rifle with
a telescopic sight on the lawn of her home. The SWAT
team had handled the crisis without firing a shot.

School principal Burton Wragg and custodian Mike
Suchar both died while eight students and officer Robb
survived their wounds. For placing aside his own safety
and going directly into a sniper's line of fire to save the
lives of innocent children, Officer Robb would be awarded
the Department's Medal for Valor.

* * * * *

As the years passed, the police SWAT unit was called
to apprehend suspects or defuse potentially volatile
incidents.

One came the night of September 14, 1984, when San
Diego police officers, Kimberly Tonahill and Timothy
Ruopp were shot to death in Balboa Park.

(Courtesy San Diego Police Museum)

San Diego SWAT officers captured their killer, Joselito Cinco the next day in a Golden Hill ravine. Cinco was convicted of their murders and sentenced to death but hung himself in San Quentin's Death Row.

(Courtesy KFMB-TV)

Other SWAT incidents involved bank robberies and domestic disputes that turned into armed hostage situations. There was no pattern to where the episodes happened. It could be North Park, Paradise Hills or Lindbergh Field but nearly all ended with a suspect in custody or sometimes death by suicide.

* * * * *

The most defining moment for the San Diego Police SWAT unit began just before 4 P.M. on Wednesday, July 18, 1984 when a deranged 41-year-old man entered a McDonald's restaurant and murdered 21 men, women, children and babies. Earlier, on the way out of his house, James Huberty told his wife and daughter, "I'm going hunting for humans and I won't be back."

James Huberty
(Courtesy KFMB-TV)

Wearing camouflage pants and a maroon T-shirt, he walked into a McDonald's restaurant with a long-barreled Uzi, a pump-action shot gun, a .9mm pistol and a cloth bag filled with ammunition. He shouted, "Freeze! Everybody down!" and began killing people. He would fire more than 245 rounds.

It could not have happened at a worse place or a worse time. The massacre was along the U.S-Mexican border at San Ysidro, an isolated three-square mile suburb 15 miles from downtown San Diego.

(Courtesy KFMB-TV)

Lieutenant Jerry Sanders, who would become Chief of Police nine years later, was the SWAT commander at the time, but he was 23 miles away in Mission Valley at a birthday party when notified of the shootings.

Jerry Sanders
(Courtesy S.D. P.O.A.)

The first of many calls to police was made at 4 P.M. but the dispatcher mistakenly sent responding officers to another McDonald's two miles away. Within ten minutes, the first officer on the correct scene was Miguel Rosario a SWAT-trained officer who thought an accidental shooting had taken place.

Miguel Rosario
(Courtesy S.D.P.O.A.)

When he arrived Rosario saw a man, Huberty, with an Uzi across his chest, open a side door of the restaurant. Rosario ducked behind a parked pickup truck before Huberty fired about 30 armor-piercing rounds at the officer who heard them slamming into metal posts and zinging off the black top.

Later, Rosario would say how inadequate he felt. "He's got an Uzi, I've got a .38, and I'm thinking it's a robbery gone bad and his buddies are going to encircle me."

When he took in the whole scene outside the restaurant he saw people hiding behind cars in the parking lot and didn't know what was going on but "I got that little sick feeling in the pit of my stomach," he said.

From behind the truck, Rosario radioed in a Code 10, "send SWAT"—and moments later a Code 11, "send everybody."

Rosario scampered back to his car to get his Ruger Mini-14 military-style rife. Two patrol officers fired shotguns to cover Rosario while he positioned himself, but he could not get a clear shot.

At 4:12 P.M., a 60-member SWAT team was dispatched but was not fully deployed and in position until 4:55 P.M.

(Courtesy KFMB-TV)

In rush hour traffic, even with lights and sirens, Sanders, who had taken time to change from civilian clothes into his uniform, was far from the scene. Minutes and lives were being lost. Three miles away, while monitoring police radio, Sanders heard field commander Lieutenant Roy Blackledge had issued the order giving sharpshooters a green light to open fire on Huberty.

Roy Blackledge
(Courtesy S.D.P.O.A)

Sanders radioed an order countermanding Blackledge
later saying he did that to prepare other officers to move in,
in case the suspect was not killed on the first shot.

Jerry Sanders
(Courtesy San Diego Police Museum)

When Sanders arrived on the scene at 5:13 P.M., more
than an hour after the initial call, he gave a "green light"
order and four minutes later a police sharpshooter, Charles
Foster, positioned on a post office roof and armed with a
Remington .308-caliber rifle, focused his scope on
Huberty's maroon shirt right above the heart.

Chuck Foster
(Courtesy San Diego Police Museum and KFMB-TV)

Foster squeezed the trigger once and sent a bullet into
Huberty's chest. The slug severed the aorta just under his
heart, and ripped through his spine, leaving an exit wound
one inch square and sending him sprawling backwards
onto the floor directly in front of the service counter,
killing him within seconds.

(Courtesy KFMB-TV)

(Courtesy KFMB-TV)

Sanders later said until that moment the police marksman could not get a clear sighting of Huberty because of shattered glass and sun reflections.

(Courtesy KFMB-TV)

The first police call to the final shot took 77 minutes. Twenty-two people (including the killer) were dead and 19 people wounded. Controversy and contradictions have lingered for years about when all of those killed actually died.

(Courtesy KFMB-TV)

That night police chief Bill Kolender with Homicide
Lieutenant Paul Ybarrondo and Mayor Roger Hedgecock
by his side, spoke to the media.

(Courtesy KFMB-TV)

Kolender said that any effort by officers to rush the restaurant or to force out the gunman with tear gas would have resulted in the deaths of several officers.

"We would have had dead cops," he said.

In addition, he said more deaths might have occurred among the 11 wounded victims inside the McDonald's, the seven other wounded people outside the restaurant and the nine people who escaped unharmed.

(Courtesy KFMB-TV)

The following week, the police said that most of the deaths occurred within 10 minutes after Huberty entered the restaurant, something disputed by others.

(Courtesy KFMB-TV)

"He was shooting people up until the point he was killed," Ronald Herrera, 33, told *The San Diego Union*, in an article published four days after the massacre. Herrera's wife, Blythe, and son, Matao, were killed in the shootings. Herrera, who suffered multiple bullet wounds, was quoted by *The Union* as saying he was shot in the first 15 minutes and "again 45 minutes later."

* * * * *

One of the police officers on the scene in San Ysidro was Commander Larry Gore, once a sergeant on the department's first anti-sniper team in the late 1960's.

Larry Gore
(Courtesy S.D.P.O.A)

His assignment July 18, 1984 was to handle the media, a herculean challenge considering news outlets responded from all over the world. It was nothing like the media response the day of the Hub Loans shootout 19 years earlier when there were no cellular telephones/cameras or instant live television coverage.

At San Ysidro a small airplane flew overhead that gave traffic reports for local radio and television stations. In the plane was Monica Zech who wrote about that day for the publication *OB Rag* in 2004.

"I looked down and could see people ducking for cover and there was a fire truck there with everybody behind it," she recalled. She saw two boys on the ground near their bicycles after being shot dead by Huberty.

Circling at 3,000 feet, Zech alerted authorities to close nearby Interstate 5 and the Tijuana border crossing a few blocks away to keep drivers from heading straight into the fire zone.

Zech was still airborne when a police shot took Huberty down. She saw firefighters and paramedics, jumping over the low walls and rushing inside to save those who were still alive.

One of the survivors wounded was McDonald's employee, 16-year-old Alberto Leos who was shot four times.

(Courtesy KFMB-TV)

Leos said moments before Huberty came in, he shot three children outside who had ridden their bikes to the restaurant. Once inside, he fired his gun in the ceiling and shouted "Everyone get down!" When the restaurant manager confronted Huberty he shot and killed her. Leos then ducked behind the counter and was there for 40 minutes trying to comfort coworkers as the gunman went through the restaurant, executing people. When he stopped to reload, Leos crawled to the basement and got into a small closet with other employees. Later he remembered saying a quick prayer. The words were: "God, give me the strength to get through this to see my family one more time. If you keep me here and give me s second chance at life I'm going to do something good with my life."

Leos said after losing so much blood he became weak and took his shoelaces off and used them as tourniquets to keep from bleeding to death. He also stuffed a rag in his mouth to keep from crying out in pain as he was hiding.

Leos spent three months in the hospital and had five surgeries that were followed by two years of physical therapy.

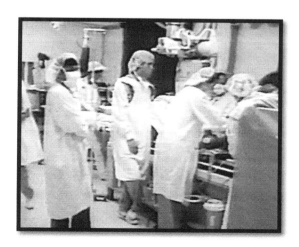

(Courtesy KFMB-TV)

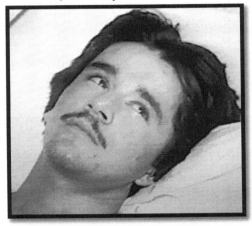

(Courtesy KFMB-TV)

Because of his wounds, Leos lost a partial football scholarship to San Jose State University.

* * * * *

Alberto Leos, against the wishes of some family members, eventually became a San Diego police officer. He said he carried angry, guilty feelings that he was not able to save his friends and coworkers. But eleven years later in 1995, Leos achieved a measure of redemption when he pulled a man from a burning car on his way to work. Leos suffered burns; some that went over the scars of his gunshot wounds. For his actions, Leos was awarded the department's life saving medal.

Leos rose through the ranks and in 2016 was promoted to Captain.

Alberto Leos
(Courtesy San Diego Police Museum)
* * * * *

Miguel Rosario, the first officer on the scene of the mass murder in 2016 was named Chief of the Bureau of Investigations for the San Diego County District Attorney.

Miguel Rosario
(Courtesy S.D.P.O.A and San Diego County District Attorney)

Many lessons were learned from the San Ysidro tragedy. A year later, San Diego police created its Special Response Team (SRT), a full-time SWAT unit. Drills are conducted in sound stages at "Strategic Operations," a production studio in Kearny Mesa owned by Stu Segall who used the studio to film television shows.

The sound stages have movable walls that allow instructors to alter the layout for each exercise that includes dynamic entries and covert clearings; all viewed and critiqued from a catwalk, by fellow SRT members. And for full production value, they sometimes play the theme music from the 1970's television series S.W.A.T.

* * * * *

Certainly the most bizarre event involving the San Diego Police Department's SWAT unit that brought worldwide attention happened on May 17, 1995 when a 35-year-old San Diego man, U.S. Army veteran and unemployed plumber, Shawn Nelson stole a 63-ton M60 World War II Patton tank from a U.S. National Guard Armory in San Diego.

Detective Howard LaBore was the first police officer to spot the tank and at first didn't think anything was out of the ordinary. "I thought it was just a tank being moved by the army until I saw him run over some cars."

Nelson went on a 23-minute rampage through the streets of a Claremont neighborhood, running over road signs, breaking off a fire hydrant that sent a geyser of water in the air, flattening a pickup truck, shredding a recreational vehicle and knocking over traffic lights.

(Courtesy KFMB-TV)

He then drove the tank onto southbound Interstate 805 and tried to knock down a bridge by running into its supports but gave up after he failed to topple it with the first few hits.

(Courtesy San Diego Police Museum and Tom Keck)

Nelson then headed south on 805 to Highway 163. Just before Genesee Avenue when he tried to crash through a cement median barrier and cross into on coming northbound traffic, the tank threw a tread and became stuck. Officers Paul Paxton and Richard Piner and Detective LaBore, climbed on top of the tank to try and get Nelson out.

(Courtesy KFMB-TV)

Since Paxton was a gunnery sergeant with the Marine Corps Reserves and a former tank driver, he was able to open the tank's hatch were he could see Nelson still working the controls. The three officers yelled for Nelson to give up but he said nothing and began rocking the tank back and forth in an attempt to free it from the median.

It was then that Paxton's partner, Richard Piner, leaned in and shot Nelson in the shoulder. The three officers reached into the tank to bring Nelson out for medical assistance. He was pulled from the tank but died at a nearby hospital the next day.

Reporters would learn that four years earlier, Nelson's wife had divorced him. A year later both his parents died of cancer and he was addicted to methamphetamine. His

plumbing equipment was stolen and with no income, his
utilities were cut off and the house was in foreclosure. A
month before he stole the tank, his live-in girlfriend died
from a drug overdose. In his backyard, investigators found
that Nelson was digging a 15-feet deep shaft, telling others
he was mining for gold.

Questions were asked about the need for police to shoot
Nelson.

Captain Tom Hall
(Courtesy S.D.P.O.A)

Captain Tom Hall handled the investigation and said
that if Nelson had managed to free the tank, he could have
taken out at least 35 vehicles that were passing at that
moment. And rather than using tear gas, that might have
stopped Nelson, but not the tank, officers would not have
been able to enter the tank if it were still mobile with tear
gas present.

In a 2018 interview, Hall's daughter Lisa who worked
for the police department's Human Resources and Crime
Lab from 1990-1994 said she was with her father and
mother at their home the afternoon the tank was stolen.
Her father and mother, Shirley and Lisa were watching the

story unfold on television and she recalls her father
shouting at the TV, "Don't shoot! Don't shoot!" As soon
as officer Richard Piner shot Shawn Nelson, Lisa Hall says
her father's pager went off. He then went to the scene and
later handled the investigation according to protocol with
an officer-involved shooting.

In the following photo taken after A.D. Brown retired,
you wonder if he and the late Tom Hall shared a few
stories about the SWAT team's actions stopping the tank
rampage on that afternoon in 1995 and what took place at
the Hub shootout 30 years earlier.

Allen Brown and Tom Hall
(Courtesy Bob Lampert)
* * * * *

Even with the bulletproof van purchased by the police
department seven months after A.D. Brown retired in 1974,
nothing in the police arsenal could have stood up to the
commandeered World War II tank. Several reports from

the scene that day were that officials considered asking for help from the Marine Corps at nearby Camp Pendleton and that an Air Wing had a Cobra helicopter armed with TOW missiles in the event they got an order from Washington.

* * * * *

While A.D. Brown had to scrimp and scrounge to equip his original ASP team (renamed SWAT), in some ways things have not changed. For several years, a 1984 bread truck was converted into a vehicle to transport SWAT equipment and personnel to police scenes and carry officers issuing high-risk warrants.

(Courtesy San Diego Police Museum)

When it broke down on the way to serve a warrant, the department replaced the bread truck with a rapid deployment vehicle that could load up to 22 people in full gear.

The team often relies on hand-me-down military gear, but this gear tends to be well used and out-of-date. And while the city of San Diego has increased training for special units and approved the purchase of more powerful firearms to better equip police to deal with deadly confrontations, much-needed assistance comes from private donations.

(Courtesy San Diego Police Museum)

Citizens for SWAT was created in 2005 to ensure that the San Diego SWAT team is equipped with the most up-to-date and effective equipment and to ensure the continued safety of San Diego citizens. They donate equipment such as vehicles, weapons, personal protection and new technology.

It was the brainchild of former SWAT Commanding Officer, now retired, Ray Shay.

Ray Shay
(Courtesy Bob Lampert)

After watching one of his officers hold a flashlight alongside his AR-15 rifle while trying to climb a fence in a high-risk situation, he went to his superiors about improving the level of his team's equipment. The response was "well Ray, it sounds like you need to have a bake sale."

Years later an annual golf tournament proved to be better moneymakers than bake sales. Citizens For SWAT has raised more than a million dollars for the SWAT unit.

"We're just a gap filler, we like to equip them with sophisticated equipment, to not only keep themselves safe but citizens as well," said Tom Schwiebert who was in the 1984 bread truck when it broke down.

Requests for equipment updates come with high price tags.

(Courtesy San Diego Police Museum)

Ultra-modern bulletproof shields, used when advancing upon armed gunmen like James Huberty at San Ysidro are nearly $4,000 each. Wheeled robots that go into buildings first can cost up to $25,000 apiece.

"If it's an empty place, we don't want to use (tear) gas and waste hours of time on an empty house we're not sure the person's there, so we throw a robot in to clear it," said Lt. Mark Saunders.

(Courtesy KGTV)

(Courtesy The Informant)

In addition to SWAT call outs, the Sniper Team has assisted U.S. Secret Service and other U.S., state and foreign government agencies with VIP (counter-sniper) security since Ronald Reagan was president. There have been dignitary protection details for presidents, vice presidents, first ladies and foreign presidents.

(Courtesy The Informant)

The Sniper Team has provided "over-watch security" for two Super Bowls, MLB World Series, local peace officer memorial services, line-of-duty funerals and high profile prisoner escorts.

Participation on the SWAT Sniper Team is collateral duty and team members are spread throughout the city. A minimum of two years on SWAT is required before applying to the Sniper Team. When team openings occur, applicants complete an interview and are tested on their marksmanship fundamentals, as well as their tactical shooting skills while under physical stress.

Those applicants making the top cut (usually six to eight) are invited to attend a Sniper Academy. The instruction lasts one week and involves training with the team's primary weapon, a scoped .308 caliber bolt-action rifle. Once on the team, members rarely leave, usually due to promotion or retirement.

(Courtesy San Diego Police Museum)
* * * * *

Allen D. Brown would likely be amazed and proud of what his Anti Sniper Platoon has evolved into. And with that said, if you had to pick one person who is the most admired police officer in the history of the San Diego Police Department, there is a compelling case to be made for Allen D. Brown.

(Courtesy Bob Lampert)

Courageous, professional, committed, loyal, compassionate, charismatic and a visionary with a great sense of humor, Lieutenant Brown had all of that and more.

Fellow police officer Lee Vaughn spoke for many who worked with Brown when he said, "He was one of the most important men in my life."

Dave Hall, a member of the first ASP team said the Hub incident set in motion a series of changes that would later define how police react to life-threatening confrontations.

Dave Hall
(Courtesy S.D.P.O.A.)

Fifty-three years after the Hub Loans and Jewelry shootout, Hall has his own "what if" and wonders, "What if A.D. Brown had not been on the scene?" Hall believes Brown's presence more than any other person put in motion changes that brought about the police department we see today.

(Courtesy Brown family)

Allen D. Brown retired from the police department in 1974 after serving 26 years on the Thin Blue Line. Following his retirement in 1980, he was invited back to show films of the 1965 Hub shootout to a class of SWAT trainees and give reflections on what happened and what should have been done differently.

"We should have isolated the building," he said candidly. "We shouldn't have moved so closely upon it, and there shouldn't have been as much firing."

But on that rainy morning there wasn't time for "should's" or "shouldn't's". There was no manual for what they faced. No simulated exercises or training sessions. Police just had to *do* it.

Brown's advice to the young officers, "Be careful, be tough and learn a lot."

Agreeing with Brown was the late deputy police chief
Ken O'Brien, who was involved in the shootout. In an
interview, O'Brien said what happened outside the Hub on
April 8, 1965 would have been handled differently in the
years that followed so that a shootout would have been a
last resort.

"It became kind of a fiasco," O'Brien said, "but it was
the best we could do."

O'Brien said that today the Special Weapons and
Tactics (SWAT) team would have been called and better
equipped to ascertain how many gunmen there were.
During the Hub shootout, police were never sure of the
number of gunmen.

"Today," O'Brien said for the interview, "we have
much better visual capabilities, such as scopes, and the
SWAT team would first gather information on the building
structure, to determine entry routes. They'd develop and
entry team to go in. There wouldn't be a shootout."

* * * * *

Current San Diego police officer Steve Willard, who is
vice president of the San Diego Police Museum, shared a
story that encapsulates the legend Allen Brown was and
remains today.

Willard remembers, "In 2005 the police museum held a
black tie gala and he (A.D. Brown) was awarded a medal
for valor for what he did at the Hub Loans shootout.

(Courtesy The Informant and San Diego Police Museum)

"Here he was, an 85-year-old man shuffling to the stage. He gets up there to accept his medal and we whispered to him, 'You have 30 seconds to say something if you like.'

(Courtesy The Informant)

"He looked at the crowd and said, 'People always ask me if I was scared that day. I'm a WWII veteran. I wasn't scared. I was pissed off. That guy had my men pinned down and someone needed to take him out. So I took him out.' Then he walked off the stage. The entire crowd was on its feet cheering. It was awesome!"

* * * * *

Allen Dale Brown can correctly be called "old school." Late in his career, in the 1970's, looking back on his life, he offered thoughts to a *San Diego Union* reporter.

"It's the in-thing in our society to dabble with what's been out for so long," Brown said during a discussion of sexual promiscuity, marijuana and the youthful attack on American institutions. The reporter wrote that Brown believed he couldn't stop what he saw as wrong.

"We are only able to enforce the laws the way our society wants them enforced," he said at the time. "This is unfortunate."

The reporter opined that Brown lamented what others may cheer and believed he was left sensing a crumbling of society and not being able to fight it. The reporter wrote that Brown believed the law has been perverted to favor the criminal.

"Part of this is the trend to so-called rehabilitation," he said.

"When a man gets out of prison they do everything but give him a federal job and a guaranteed wage."

The reporter asked Brown about the theory that society is somehow responsible for a man's crime. His only one printable response: "Ridiculous!"

Few people had Brown's perspective on the death penalty. Robert Anderson murdered Louis Richards and then later when Brown and Anderson faced each other, Anderson would have shot the police officer had not the pistol been loaded with the wrong ammunition. In

Anderson's case, Brown believed the reversal of the death penalty in California was not administered properly.

"Punishment should be swift and sure."

And he believed that punishment should fit the crime.

"My feelings depend on the type of crime the man commits. You get a child molester and I think he should be desexualized.

"When you get somebody who severely beats someone else, you wish he could be flogged.

"You know it isn't right and maybe in the final analysis you wouldn't want it to happen, but you almost wish he could experience the pain he inflicted on someone else."

The reporter's story noted that Brown was a popular instructor at Miramar College where he taught criminal law. Brown was also characterized as being a cop who was scrupulously honest and hard driving but looking at the world he had fought so hard for and wondering, now and again, if it was all worthwhile.

"We have improved," he said of police attitudes, "but when I say that I don't mean to demean the rough-tough old-timers. There was a place for them, and they were good—then. But they would be very unacceptable today."

The reporter wrote that "compared with cops hired primarily for their size and ability to knock other people about, Brown rates as a screaming liberal. Even among the present breed, he considers himself progressive."

"I believe," he said, "I'm driving in the new direction, but the old hardline can't be ruled out.

"I've changed with the times, but have taken with me the ability to come on rather strong when that's required."

Brown told the reporter that policemen are a fairly conservative lot.

"Maybe because they see so many things in life, they

see the results of liberal thinking."

Brown then compared swift social change with the old Hudson Terraplane—"a big, swanky thing. It was too far in advance of its time and it wasn't accepted. Changes have to come slowly."

1935 Hudson Terraplane Six Suburban Sedan
(Photo credit: Hemmings.com)

At the time of the article, Brown noted that law enforcement was caught up in the midst of a social upheaval that was shaking society to its roots.

"Our world is getting growing pains and our society has been unable to keep up with its own growth."

The newspaper story told of Allen Brown's older brother, Frank. Perhaps because the family had lived in the Philippines (Brown's father was an Army medical corps captain), but Frank Brown requested Army infantry duty there.

He was captured during World War II and survived the Bataan death march, only to be blown out of the water as he and other prisoners were being taken to a Japanese POW camp.

In 1944, the year his brother, Frank was killed, A.D. Brown entered the Army and after officers candidate school he became a second lieutenant, trained recruits in Texas for three months and then was flown to Okinawa where he saw combat as a platoon leader.

He later joined the 11th Airborne and served nine months with the occupation forces in Japan.

When A.D. Brown joined the San Diego Police Department in 1948, he walked a beat for two weeks before attending the police academy. His salary as a rookie cop was $211 a month. His monthly paycheck as a lieutenant was $1,343.

(Courtesy: Brown family)

Up until the Hub shootout, other than at the police firing range, A.D. Brown had never used a pistol or a rifle while on duty and after April 8, 1965, never fired one again. And his son, Frank, except for the firing range, never used a weapon on duty in his four years as a police officer.

A.D. Brown and son, Frank, 2006, a year before A.D.'s passing
(Courtesy Bob Lampert)

Part of A.D. Brown's legacy was the creation of the Police Department's Community Relations Division. Largely in response to what they saw happen in the 1965 Los Angeles riots in Watts, Brown, Bill Kolender and Lieutenant Bill Gore, teamed to put into action a way for the department to build better relationships with citizens in each city neighborhood.

Kolender, who received his training from Brown and went on to become San Diego police chief and San Diego County sheriff said that Brown "was the best instructor and had a way of teaching young men and women how to care about their jobs, care about the people they dealt with and how to do their jobs professionally."

Bill Kolender as a police officer and Police Chief
(Courtesy San Diego Police Museum)

Bill Kolender sworn in by Judge Frank Brown (son of
Allen D. Brown) as sheriff in 1995
(Courtesy San Diego Police Museum & San Diego County
Sheriff)

"He showed hundreds of San Diego police officers how
to be successful in their jobs, including me."

Chapter 16
The Corner of Fifth Avenue & F Street

The building where the Hub shootout took place and the surrounding area looked much different in 2018 than it did on April 8, 1965, beginning with the southeast corner of Fifth Avenue and F Street.

In 1920, Levis Brinton, a Pennsylvania farmer who had moved to San Diego in 1887 built a five-story hotel at Fifth and F. It opened as the Oxford Hotel but around 1930 his widow Florence changed the name to the Hotel William Penn, likely as a tribute to the founder of the English colony of Pennsylvania in 1682.

The hotel was advertised as "the only first-class hotel in the hub of the amusement and shopping district" and occupied the top four floors and leased two tenant spaces below including a basement. One of the first businesses on the ground floor (where the Hub Loans and Jewelry Company would eventually be located) was the Foerster Drug Company, once the only all night drug store in San Diego.

Later, the corner of Fifth and F was the home of Mr. O's Liquors but when the William Penn Building was sold and renovated, the liquor store closed in January 1990.

A year later, in 1991, Maloney's Tavern opened its doors and in 2000, the property above the bar was turned into a mixed-use development with 18 residential units and two retail anchor tenants. Maloney's tavern with two entrances on F Street and Fifth Avenue continued but the old Hub space remained vacant.

Then years later the corner's two floors were refurbished and became a Starbucks Coffee House. There was a loft on the second floor mezzanine where Ted Swienty played "possum" under a bed while hiding from Robert Anderson.

In early 2008, the William Penn Hotel was sold for $7.5 million and on July 27, 2014, Starbucks closed its store and a new tenant prepared to occupy the space where gunshots echoed on April 8, 1965. The short-lived tenant would be the Orso Art Gallery.

In the summer of 2015, the William Penn Building was sold again to a Beverly Hills company for $10.2 million cash. Orso Art Gallery would go out of business while Maloney's hung on as the sole anchor tenant. But the bar, whose owners were having problems at other locations in Denver, Flagstaff and Tucson for failing to pay rent, taxes, and other fees, had become tired and run down. In 2016 Maloney's Tavern served its last drink.

Enter a company called Brethren Collective. It stepped in to lease the two-level space with plans to invest heavily for a complete makeover.

The result was a new Gaslamp Quarter attraction, Queensborough, named after New York City's largest district. In the summer of 2017, the swanky 1,800 square feet cocktail bar and dining room opened on the first floor.

Months later the subterranean part of the building opened with a 6,000 square foot upscale lounge complete with a library-setting and nightclub alternative to patrons.

It looked good on paper and even better in person. But while the amenities and atmosphere were without equal, there was one problem: not enough people bothered to see it in person.

The Queensborough closed for good on March 24, 2018.

* * * * *

As for the William Penn, at the time of the Hub shootout, it was a seedy, rundown hotel. But now, the building offers 18 individual one-bedroom apartments in a secure setting on the top four floors that rent for about $2,000 a month.

* * * * *

In 2018, a new business was planned to occupy the once bullet-riddled walls that housed the Hub Loans & Jewelry Company.

(Courtesy KGTV, KFMB-TV and San Diego Police Museum)

In August 2018, the two floors were being readied for a Tacos El Gordo restaurant. Plans for the 2,200 square foot area, once the target for bullets and tear gas included a kitchen, serving line, tables and other restaurant amenities.

Construction worker Matt Weingart stands in the entrance where Louis Richards fell after being shot.

Inside, is the stairway where Hub clerk Ted Swienty fled to escape from Robert Anderson and the 900 square-foot mezzanine where Swienty hid in a room for four hours before Sergeant Allen Brown and his men scaled the steps and shot the suspect.

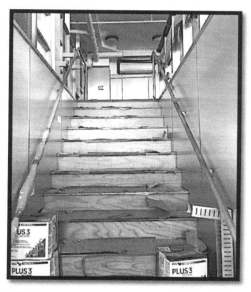

   The corner outside that once housed the Hub and was
under siege by police on April 8, 1965, fifty-three years
later bares little evidence of the violence that went on for
four hours. Despite up to a thousand bullets that were shot
into the building and the two hand grenades that were
tossed into the Hub, not many visible signs are left of what
happened. The few that remain are on the north side of the
building along F Street.

(Courtesy KGTV, KFMB-TV and San Diego Police
Museum)

The largest evidence of the firefight is a hole gouged out of cement from a bullet that missed its mark. And next to the chipped out crater is a weathered spider web, caked with dust that has survived for who knows how long.

Chapter 17
The Times

The 1960's have been called a decade that changed America and was the most turbulent era in American history. With 1965 right in the middle, this is what life was like on April 8, 1965:

In the early morning hours before Louis Richards went to work or Robert Anderson decided to get on a bus, thousands of copies of *The San Diego Union* newspaper were tossed on driveways all over San Diego County.

The paper's headline was **Johnson Shifts Policy, Asks Viet Nam Talks**. The words did not match reality because the war in South Viet Nam was ramping up. The United States was rapidly increasing its military forces since it was apparent the South Vietnamese government could not hold back North Viet Nam and Viet Cong forces. In April 1965, more than 30,000 American military forces were in South Viet Nam and another 20,000 were on the way.

American war-related deaths in 1964 had been 206. When 1965 was over, 1,863 American troops would die.

Also on the front page on April 8 was a photograph of 46-year-old Gustav C. Hertz, a kidnaped U.S. aid officer who vanished on a motorbike trip near Saigon February 2. He was the chief public administrator for the U.S. Agency for International Development's mission in Viet Nam.

The Viet Cong were threatening to kill Hertz if Saigon authorities executed a terrorist arrested in the bombing of the U.S. Embassy March 30 that killed 22 people. The Viet Cong saboteur was 33-year-old Nguyen Van Thai.

(Hertz was held for two years and died of malaria in a North Vietnamese prison.)

At the same time, Russia's Premier Alexi N. Kosygin accused the United States of barbarism and crimes against humanity in Viet Nam and predicted "peace-loving nations will never forgive the American imperialists."

Tensions were also high in Europe. In the upper left hand corner of the *Union's* front page on April 8, 1965 was a story about swarms of Russian jet fighters roaring over West Berlin and firing blank cannon ammunition and buzzing the mall where West Germany's parliament was meeting. Germany was still divided in two and East German Communists were blocking all traffic on the Berlin autobahn for three straight days. Their reason for the action was a protest that the West German parliament had no right to meet in West Berlin because the city is not part of West Germany.

Closer to home in the middle of the *Union's* page 1 was a photograph of teachers and students at St. Charles Elementary and Marian Catholic High School in South San Diego at 18th Street. They were shown being led by Sister Mary Lillian and Reverend Benjamin Carrier crossing a muddy area on planks. The day before a rain-soaked San Diego had received another half-inch of rain, making the month the wettest April in 14 years. More rain was predicted for the day and as was experienced between 10 AM. And 2 P.M. at Fifth and F, there were many downpours.

In sports, April 8 would be the first round of the Masters golf classic at Augusta, Georgia and 25-year-old Jack Nicklaus was a 4-1 favorite to win his second Masters' title in three years. When the tournament ended on Sunday, Nicklaus ran away from the field with a four-day score of 271, 17 under par, which was a record at that time and nine shots better than Arnold Palmer and Gary Player who tied for second. San Diegan Gene Litler finished tied for sixth. First-place money was $20,000, compared with just under $2 million for the 2018 winner.

On April 8, 1965 the minimum wage was $1.25. This is equivalent to $9.88 in 2018 dollars. A trip to the supermarket in 1965 would have ground beef and chicken at 33¢ a pound; cantaloupes were four for $1, tuna 25¢ a can, a 15-ounce loaf of bread was 27¢, a 26-ounce bottle of syrup was 29¢ and a giant box of Ajax detergent was 49¢. A pair of leather shoes for a man was $9 and a wool suit $59.95.

In 1965 the average cost of a new home was $13,600, a new car $2,650 and gasoline was 31¢ a gallon. The 1965 Volkswagen Bug sold for $1,675. The average income for the year was $6,450.

On April 8, a Lucky Lager beer truck parked inside the Coke truck at the Hub shootout served as a cover for police officers.

(Courtesy KGTV, KFMB-TV and San Diego Police Museum)

Lucky Lager, first brewed in San Francisco was launched as "One of the World's Finest Beers." By 1937, it was California's second best-selling beer. In 1965 the beer was in its heyday but in the next ten years just as the area around the Hub would deteriorate, Lucky Lager under the ownership of Pabst Brewing Company and Canadian Labatt Brewing, became a beer looked upon with disdain by serious beer drinkers.

* * * * *

Cellular telephones in 1965 were as far-fetched a dream as Dick Tracy watches.

(Courtesy KGTV, KFMB-TV and San Diego Police Museum)

In the area around the Hub shootout, as an officer brought new supplies of ammunition, signs along the sidewalk alerted people that there were pay telephones inside.

Computers were in their infancy and the baby was huge. In 1965, computers had mainframes the size of refrigerators, sometimes filling up entire rooms. A year earlier at the 1964 New York World Fair, Olivetti had unveiled its prototype desktop computer, the Programma 101. It weighed 78 pounds and stored its memory on magnetic cards and had no display screen. It used a small printer and a roll of paper about 3 1/2 inches wide. Priced at $3,200, the company sold 40,000 units.

On June 15, 1965, the local front page of the *San Diego Union* reported the beginning of Robert Anderson's murder trial in downtown San Diego. To the left of that story was news about a computer to be used at the San Diego Coast Guard Air Station. The computerized Automatic Merchant Vessel Reporting System (AMVER) would begin operating in the fall in the Pacific area from a center in San Francisco and aid in search and rescue operations.

The next day the *San Diego Union* reported that seventeen U.S. Coast Guard cutters sent to Viet Nam to halt the smuggling of arms to Communist forces might eventually be given to the Vietnamese.

* * * * *

In 1965, San Diego looked like a Navy town because sailors were forbidden from carrying civilian clothes aboard ships. That meant when large ships were in port, the streets were flooded with sailors in uniform. Ships that anchored in the bay would use liberty boats to shuttle sailors to the Broadway pier at the foot of downtown and hundreds, sometimes thousands of white hats would make their way to the Gaslamp Quarter. Five years later, the Navy changed its policy and allowed sailors to have civilian clothes on their ships to be worn on liberty.

* * * * *

The Hub Loans & Jewelry Company shootout was the big story on television beginning April 8 and took people's attention from the normal TV fare of that time. In 1962, network news had expanded from 15 minutes to 30 minutes each night and in April 1965 the big three were anchored by Walter Cronkite on CBS, Chet Huntley and David Brinkley on NBC and Peter Jennings on ABC.

Popular programs of that time were Perry Mason, Dr. Kildare, My Three Sons and Carl Reiner's The Celebrity Game Show.

Entertainment on the big screen included "My Fair Lady" and "Mary Poppins."

Popular comic strips each day were Dick Tracy, Peanuts, Lil' Abner and Little Orphan Annie.

On April 8, 1965 the sports page reported the Baltimore Bullets' first victory after two losses in the seven-game National Basketball Association playoffs, a 122-115 win over the Los Angeles Lakers. Bailey Howell led the Bullets with 29 points. Jerry West matched the number on his jersey and had 44 points in the losing effort. Laker All Star Elgin Baylor was injured. Los Angeles would go on to win the series four games to two, but without Baylor for the rest of the playoffs lost in the NBA Finals to Boston four games to two.

Two years later in 1967, San Diego would get its first NBA team, the San Diego Rockets.

* * * * *

On August 28, 1965 the Beatles with John Lennon, Paul McCartney, George Harrison and Ringo Starr came to San Diego and performed a concert at Balboa Stadium. Surprisingly, at the height of "Beatlemania," the event was not sold out and just 17,013 screaming fans turned out, leaving more than 10,000 seats unoccupied.

The venue was the home of the American Football League, San Diego Chargers that came to San Diego in 1961 from Los Angeles. The team was absorbed into the National Football League in 1970 and played its games at San Diego Stadium in Mission Valley. Team owner Dean Spanos betrayed loyal Charger fans in 2017 when after 56 years in San Diego he moved the team to Los Angeles.

* * * * *

When Robert Anderson's murder trial was about to begin in June 1965, much of the nation and world focus had been on outer space. The Gemini four-day space mission 135 miles above the earth, featured astronaut Ed White floating in space for 20 minutes while watched by command pilot James McDivit. On Monday, June 7, the astronauts splashed down and after being picked up by the crew from the aircraft carrier USS Wasp, White and McDivit were invited to visit President Lyndon Johnson at his Texas ranch on Friday, a welcome diversion for the President since the war in Viet Nam was going badly. More American military men were dying and protests at home were growing louder.

* * * * *

The San Diego Evening Tribune was still publishing its evening newspaper in 1965. Fourteen years later, the paper's staff would be honored with a Pulitzer Prize in Spot News Reporting of the collision of a Pacific Southwest Airlines 737 jet and a small private plane over the city and its crash into North Park. The death toll was 144 with 135 on board Flight 182, the two people in the Cessna and seven people on the ground.

In 1992, the paper, a victim of the evening television newscasts ceased operations and merged with the morning *San Diego Union.*

* * * * *

And on April 8, 1965, America was six days away from officially remembering a national tragedy that happened 100 years earlier when President Abraham Lincoln was assassinated April 14, 1865.

Chapter 18
The Author

At the time of the Hub shootout, the author was in his second month as a U.S. Naval officer candidate at Newport Rhode Island. He had graduated in January from Arizona State University with a Bachelor of Science Degree in Business Administration. He would be commissioned an Ensign in June 1965.

For the next four years, his assignments included the USS Conflict (MSO 426) that was on Market Time patrol off the southern coast of South Viet Nam. He was then transferred to Commander Naval Forces Korea in Seoul for 13 months and then was at Naval Communications Unit, London for two years that served the Commander in Chief U.S. Navy Europe.

* * * * *

    While in Viet Nam in November 1965, he is shown holding s similar type of Thompson Sub Machine gun that Sergeant Sam Chasteen used seven months earlier in the Hub shootout.

(Courtesy KGTV, KFMB-TV and
San Diego Police Museum)

Discharged as a Lieutenant in March 1969, later that year John began a 31-year career in television news during which time he was awarded six Emmy's. His start came in June 1969 as a news writer/production assistant at KTAR-TV Channel 12, the NBC affiliate in Phoenix, Arizona. He eventually became a field reporter and news anchor there.

In 1975, after six years in Phoenix he joined the news team at KGTV Channel 10, the NBC affiliate in San Diego where he worked as a general assignment reporter and occasional news anchor.

(Courtesy Bob Lampert)

Two years later, in 1977, he was hired as a general assignment news reporter by the ABC-TV-owned station in Chicago, WLS-TV Channel 7.

(Courtesy WLS-TV)

Then in 1980 John returned to San Diego where he completed his television career with 20 years as a news anchor and field reporter at the CBS affiliate, KFMB-TV Channel 8.

(Courtesy KFMB-TV)

(Courtesy KFBM-TV)

John has firsthand experience and understands what members of the news media encountered while on the scene of the Hub shootout.

He covered the shooting deaths of two Maricopa County Sheriff's deputies in Phoenix, Arizona on January 19, 1971. Deputies Rex Stone, 51 and Warren LaRue, 56 were gunned down by 42-year-old Hector Garcia as they attempted to seize his mobile home to satisfy a $833 judgment. LaRue, who was set to retire in 60 days, was shot four times in the back and died instantly. Stone, despite being shot in the chest was able to draw his gun and fired five shots, hitting Garcia with all five, killing him. Somehow, Garcia's body ended up by the squad car's steering wheel, sprawled across the front seat. Stone then collapsed and died at the scene.

Just three weeks earlier, deputy Stone's son, Dale, a Phoenix motorcycle police officer had been killed in the line of duty while responding to an emergency call following the shooting of another officer.

* * * * *

On May 25, 1979, John was part of the news team at
WLS-TV responding to the crash of American Airlines
Flight 191 at O'Hare International Airport. The DC-10's
number one engine broke off the left wing on takeoff and
the airliner went down in a field near the airport killing
271 people on board and two on the ground. His work on
the story brought the first of six Emmy awards.

* * * * *

A month later on June 24, 1979, John was inside police
lines to cover a riot that took place outside the Great Lakes
Naval Training Center in North Chicago.

(Courtesy WLS-TV)

More than 300 rampaging sailors with bricks and rocks spilled into the nearby business district and overturned and set fire to a police cruiser. Using large stones from the railroad ballast, the sailors pelted windows in a Chicago Northwestern passenger train that was traveling north along nearby tracks.

* * * * *

John interviewed former San Diego police officer and SWAT team member Chuck Foster.

Chuck Foster
(Courtesy San Diego Police Museum)

The onetime Army Green Beret shot and killed James
Huberty after Huberty had murdered 21 men, women and
children on July 18, 1984 at a McDonald's restaurant near
the Mexican border in San Ysidro.

(Courtesy KFMB-TV)

Other than time spent on the police target range, Foster revealed to John in the interview that it was the only time in his career that he fired a weapon while on duty.

(Courtesy KFMB-TV)
* * * * *

John also was part of the news coverage during the Los Angeles riots that broke out on April 29, 1992 after the acquittals of four L.A.P.D. officers in the beating of Rodney King.

(Courtesy KFMB-TV)

(Courtesy KFMB-TV)

Five days of rioting resulted in 63 deaths, more than
two thousand injuries, more than twelve thousand arrests
and an estimated $1 billion in property damage.

Then in March 1997, John was involved in reporting
the mass suicide of 39 members of the Heaven's Gate
religious cult in Rancho Santa Fe north of San Diego.

(Courtesy KFMB-TV)

* * * * *

John worked with several of those mentioned in this book, including Ray Wilson, the news director and principle anchor at KFMB-TV who was on the air before John came to Channel 8 in 1980.

Courtesy KFMB-TV

Also while on the news team at KGTV, Channel 10 in 1975, John worked with photographer Art Farian who was interviewed for this book.

(Courtesy Bob Lampert)

He also worked with the late Bob Craft who was filming at the Hub scene.

(Courtesy Alvida Craft)

And he was a colleague of the late Jack Moorhead who became the assignment editor at KGTV, but was on the scene filming the Hub Loans & Jewelry Company shootout for KOGO-TV (later the station became KGTV).

(Courtesy Bob Lampert)

While at KGTV, John worked with news photographer Bob Lampert who was out of town on another assignment the day of the Hub shootout. Bob helped in the research and photographs for this book and was a key resource for contacting people linked to the Hub incident.

Bob Lampert, 1964 at GOP convention in San Francisco
(Courtesy KGTV and Bob Lampert)

* * * * *

Carl Gilman, who was first on the scene of the Hub
shootout for KFMB-TV and was interviewed for this book
was a competitor of John's in 1975-1976 while John was
at KGTV before Gilman left Channel 8 in 1976.

(Courtesy Carl Gilman)

Chapter 19

In Memoriam

(In order of mention)

Frank W. Morales, July 20, 1933 – June 6, 1993
   Navy Petty Officer Frank Wenceslao Morales
volunteered to throw two concussion grenades into the
Hub Loans & Jewelry building that led to the capture of
Robert Anderson. Morales served 22 years in the Navy
and reached the rank of GMG2 (Gunner's Mate Second
Class). He passed away at age 59 on June 6, 1993 in San
Diego at age 59 and is buried at Riverside National
Cemetery.

(Courtesy The Informant and *All Hands*)

In 1965, for his action at the Hub shootout Morales was awarded the Navy and Marine Corps Medal: "CITATION:
The President of the United States of America takes pleasure in presenting the Navy and Marine Corps Medal to Gunner's Mate Third Class Frank W. Morales, United States Navy, for heroism while serving at Shore Patrol Headquarters, San Diego, California, on 8 April 1965, in response to a request by the San Diego Police Department for Shore Patrol assistance. A gunman had shot and killed one of the employees in a store, and was still in the building engaged in a gunfight with police. After several hours of gunfire, use of tear gas and other police methods had failed to dislodge the gunman from his position, Gunner's Mate Third Class Morales volunteered to throw concussion grenades into the building. At the risk of his life, Gunner's Mate Third Class Morales approached the store and hurled a grenade into the first-floor entrance, followed by another grenade into the upstairs portion of the building. After the explosion of the second grenade, police were able to gain access to the second floor and apprehend the gunman. Gunner's Mate Third Class Morales' actions in the face of grave personal risk prevented further bloodshed and loss of life."

* * * * *

When this book was first released in September 2018, the author had been unable to locate the whereabouts of Navy Petty Officer, Frank W. Morales the gunner's mate who tossed two concussion grenades into the Hub. But one month later, my friend Andy Thompson of Poulton-le-Fylde, England solved the mystery.

Andy Thompson at Laurel & Hardy Museum
Ulverston, England (Birthplace of Stan Laurel)

Andy uncovered records that show Frank Wenceslao Morales passed away at age 59 on June 6, 1993 in San Diego.

- Louis Richards, (November 10, 1902 – April 8, 1965)

The funeral and burial for Louis Richards was April 9,
1965. The Hub manager lived at 4410 Utah Street in North
Park and was survived by his widow, Leah and a brother.
He was a member of Blackmer Masonic Lodge, The
Tifereth Israel Synagogue Men's Club and the Hebrew
Home for the Aged.
His grave is in lot 3, grave number 1 in the north portion
of the Sholom Cemetery section of Greenwood Memorial
Park in San Diego.
• 	Sam Zemen, (1914-1988) owner of the Hub Loans
and Jewelry Company. He is buried along with other
family members at Greenwood Memorial Park
Mausoleum's West Sholom Corridor not far from the
grave of Louis Richards. Zemen's wife, Myrtle passed
away in 1988 at age 72. His father, Louis, a Russian Jew
died a year before the Hub shootout at age 78.
• 	Max Zemen (1912-1963) Sam Zemen's brother,
Max passed away two years before the Hub shootout at the
age of 51. Max Zemen played softball in the Jewish
Softball League Sunday mornings at Horace Mann
playground located at Park and El Cajon Blvd.
• 	Theodore C. "Ted" Swienty, (1901-1973). The
Hub Loans and Jewelry Company clerk is buried in
Resthaven Cemetery, Iron River, Michigan. His headstone
reads "Theodore C. Swienty, California, Pvt. U.S. Army,
World War I.
• 	Lieutenant Allen D. Brown, (1920-2007), Badge
#61, San Diego Police Department 26 years and was a
resident of Del Cerro. He passed away on June 27, 2007 at
age 87 and his remains were cremated.

Allen Brown and Frank Brown 1994

In the mid-1970's, Brown started an annual December luncheon for former San Diego police officers (shown in the photo above). The event grew from a handful of officers to more than 300 in 2018 and is organized by the San Diego Police Historical Association.

• Wayne Colburn, (1916-1983), Inspector, Badge #8 & 386, San Diego Police Department 23 years. A World War II Marine veteran, Colburn passed away June 19, 1983 at age 67 and is buried at Glen Abbey Memorial Park in Bonita, California.

-     Wesley Sharp, (1899-1991) Badge #130, San Diego Police Department 36 years (Police Chief 1962-1968). He was a World War I veteran and passed away November 3, 1991 at age 93 and was buried at Fort Rosecrans National Cemetery. He said his first training in 1931, as a police officer was limited. "We lined up and a sergeant told me to walk a beat and gave me a number. I had been issued a badge, a gun and a call-box key. We marched uptown, and older policemen told me where the call boxes were located and what the beat boundaries were. That's all the training I had."

- James Biggins, Jr. (1929-2016) was Robert Anderson's defense attorney. After receiving his law degree in 1952 from Stanford University he was drafted into the U.S. Army during the Korean War and was stationed in Hawaii as a Military Police Officer.

(Courtesy Utta Biggins)

He worked in the San Diego County District Attorney's office before moving into private practice.

After passing away in 2016 at age 87 he was laid to rest at Fort Rosecrans National Cemetery.

- Chuck Woolsey, assignment editor, KOGO-TV passed away.

- Les Dodds, former news photographer at KOGO-TV, San Diego filmed at the Hub shootout and is deceased.

Les Dodds
(Courtesy Brown family)

•   Detective Sergeant Robert McLennan, (1920-2017) Badge #230 & 636 ID 1619. He was among the first on the scene at the Hub shootout and passed away at age 97.

(Courtesy San Diego Police Museum)

•   Detective William Duncan, (1934-1969) Badge #263. Early on the Hub shootout scene, Duncan exchanged fire with Robert Anderson. He was a Korean War Navy veteran and passed away after surgery at age 35. He was

buried with military honors at Mount Hope Cemetery in
San Diego

(Courtesy San Diego Police Museum)
- Captain Charles David (Dave) Crow (1932-2018)
Badge #770, 107, 35 ID 1215, San Diego Police
Department 33 years.

Billie and Dave Crow
(Courtesy Crow family)
Dave graduated from Sweetwater High School before
being drafted into the Army where he spent most of his
time overseas. After the Army, Dave joined the Postal
Service and worked as a postman in National City,
California. He became a San Diego police officer in 1956

and retired with the rank of captain. He helped create a
section in El Camino Memorial Park devoted to police and
fire department retirees. He was cremated and his ashes
scattered at sea.
•   Detective Leigh Emmerson, (1929-2006), Badge
#702, ID# 1295. A Korean War Navy veteran, Emmerson
served on the attack ship Washburn although his widow,
Kathy says he was often pulled off duty to play basketball
for the Navy.

(Courtesy San Diego Police Museum, Kathy Emmerson
and Bob Lampert)

While he was among the officers involved in wounding and apprehending Robert Anderson, Kathy Emmerson said her husband didn't talk much about the Hub shootout. Later he worked in narcotics but when he turned his attention to fingerprints, he became an expert. His hobby was collecting American cut glass and his widow says his knowledge of fingerprints enabled him to identify intricate patters in glass. This brought offers to lecture around the country. Leigh Emmerson passed away in 2006 in Ramona, California at age 76.

•   Ray Wilson, (1918-1995). A World War II Army veteran, Ray was at KFMB-TV for 35 years and passed away at age 77.

(Courtesy KFMB-TV)

•   Robert "Bob" Regan (born Aram Samuel Rejabian), (1917-2007). Bob was the 11 P.M. news anchor at KFMB-TV and an on-air personality for KGB and KCBQ radio.

(Courtesy KFMB-TV)

He was a World War II Marine veteran and attained the
rank of Major. For his heroism at Iwo Jima, Bob was
awarded the Silver Star. He passed away at age 70 and is
buried at Fort Rosecrans National Cemetery.
•   Sam Rinaker, Jr. (1913-2004). Rinaker was the
early evening news anchor at KOGO-TV (later KGTV)
Channel 10 from 1960 to 1975. He was a World War II
Army Air Corps veteran and left broadcasting in 1975 and
was Director of Public Policy at San Diego Gas & Electric
until 1984. He was killed at the age of 91 while a
passenger in a car crash March 28, 2004 in La Jolla and is
buried at El Camino Memorial in San Diego.

(Courtesy KGTV)

•   Frank Van Cleave (1931-2008) former news anchor KOGO-TV, San Diego.

Frank and Nan Van Cleave

After leaving television he lived in San Diego and worked in real estate, eventually moving to Portland, Oregon. He passed away on September 20, 2008 at age 77.

•   George Whitney (1918-1974) former vice president and general manager of KFMB-TV, San Diego from 1953-1969.

George Whitney
(Courtesy *Broadcasting 1974)*

He left the station to be general manager for Pacific Southwest Airlines (PSA) Broadcasting that had five FM radio stations and earlier was a minority stockholder for the American Football League (AFL) San Diego Chargers. He died of a heart attack at his La Jolla home on February 4, 1974 at age 66.

•   Clayton Brace (1923-1986), vice president and general manager KOGO-TV/KGTV Channel 10 in San Diego. World War II Army Signal Corps veteran passed away in 1986 at age 63.

•   Harold Keen (1912-1981), former newspaper reporter and longtime television news reporter and editorial director at KFMB-TV, San Diego. Keen in 1949 developed Channel 8's first program. In 1975, Keen lost his left leg to amputation because of circulation problems and passed away in 1981 after leg circulation surgery at age 69.

(Courtesy KFMB-TV)

(Courtesy KFMB-TV)

•   Detective Sergeant Carl Davis (1917-1986), Badge #120. He served 27 years and later became Chief of Security at Los Medanos Community College in Antioch, California until he retired in 1984. He died at his home in Camp Connell, California on December 6, 1986 at age 69.

(Courtesy San Diego Police Museum, KGTV, KFMB-TV and Bob Lampert)

- Lieutenant Robert Augustine (1928-1986) Badge
  65, 142, 498, ID 1039.

(Courtesy San Diego Police Museum)

Augustine was one of the officers who went up the stairway with Sergeant Brown to capture Robert Anderson. He served 32 years in the patrol, narcotics, Vice and public affairs sections before retiring on disability in 1983. He passed away at age 58.

- Bob Redding (1935-2005). Retired *San Diego Union* news photographer. On April 8, 1965, with gunfire all around him, Redding came to the aid of Robert Crandall after the newspaper editor suffered a fatal heart attack. Redding draped Crandall's body over his shoulder and along with officer Ed Perkins carried Crandall's body from the shootout scene. Redding was with the *San Diego Union* for 36 years and retired in 1992. He passed away from complications of a stroke in 2005 at age 70.

•   Bill Kolender, former San Diego Police Chief and San Diego County Sheriff (1935-2015), ID 0001.

Bill Kolender 2012
(Courtesy San Diego Police Museum, San Diego County and Bob Lampert)

In 1956 during his final interview before he began his career in law enforcement, Kolender met then police chief Larry Jansen. That night Jansen went home and told his wife, "Today I hired a young Jewish boy who is one day going to become the chief of police." Frances Jansen said her husband never made a comment like that before or after that day.

Kolender served as police chief from 1975 to 1988 before working for the Copley Press for three years and then as director of the California Youth Authority. In 1994 he defeated an incumbent sheriff and was reelected three times before retiring during his fourth term in 2009.

He passed away in 2015 after a long battle with Alzheimer's disease at age 80 and is buried at El Cajon Cemetery.

•   Deputy Chief Ken O'Brien (1934-2010) Badge #2 & 743, ID 1707. A U.S. Marine Corps Korean War veteran, O'Brien served 31 years with the police

department and another 20 with other agencies. He retired in 2007 to care for his ailing wife, Bennie. Ken O'Brien passed away in 2010 at age 76.
• Captain Howard Charman, Jr. (1916-2000) Badge #14, 27 & 199, San Diego Police Department 25 years. He was a Navy veteran and passed away in Escondido, California in 2000 at age 83.
• Vera Brown (1921-2011). Married 65 years to Lieutenant Allen Brown. She was active in San Diego Police Auxiliary, Shriners Ladies, and other civic organizations and passed away at age 90.

Vera and Allen Brown 1988 photo
(Courtesy San Diego Police Officers Association and The Informant)
• Detective Sergeant Lyder "Swede" Svidal (1922-1999) Badge 526. Svidal served in World War II in the Army Air Corps and was a San Diego police officer for 28 years. Svidal was one of the officers with Sergeant Brown when he captured Robert Anderson. He passed away at age 76.

(Courtesy San Diego Police Museum)
•   Lieutenant Clarence Meyers (1913-2003) Badge 35,
121 & 151. Myers was a World War II Navy veteran and
was one of the officers on the stairway with Sergeant
Brown when he captured Robert Anderson.

(Courtesy San Diego Police Museum)
The only time he fired his weapon on duty except on the
pistol range was at the Hub shootout. He passed away in
2003 at age 90.

- George Potter, former news photographer at KOGO-TV San Diego, who filmed at the Hub shootout, is deceased.

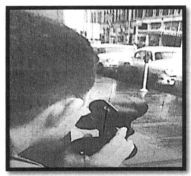

(Courtesy KGTV, KFMB-TV and San Diego Police Museum)

- Bob Craft (1932-2013), former news photographer at KOGO-TV/KGTV, San Diego who filmed at the Hub shootout. He struggled with heart issues for 40 years and passed away from a stroke in January 2013 at age 81.

(Courtesy Alvida Craft)

- Jack Moorhead (1931-2012), former news photographer who filmed at the Hub shootout and later was the assignment editor at KOGO-TV/KGTV, San

Diego. Jack was one of the most decent, caring and professional persons I ever worked with.

(Courtesy Lorraine Moorhead)

He was at Channel 10 for 30 years and passed away from complications of cancer in 2012 at age 80.

•   Ed Deverill (1917-1999), radio news reporter for KFSD/KOGO, KGB and KCBQ. The veteran newsman passed away from complications of a stroke in his Kuaii, Hawaii home at age 81.

(Courtesy KGTV, KFMB-TV and San Diego Police Museum)
A favorite story was that in 1945 he fainted on the job at a radio station in Honolulu after getting the news off the wire of President Franklin D. Roosevelt's death.
•   Captain Hugh French (1929-1999) Badge 103. Marine Corps Korean War Veteran served 23 years with SDPD.

(Courtesy Brown family and San Diego Police Museum)
After retiring from the department, French was chief of campus police at the University of California, San Diego until 1984. He passed away from a heart attack at his El Cajon home in 1999 at age 70.
•   Deputy Marshall Elwin Bunnell, Badge #379. Bunnell was involved in a shootout in1958 that at the time was the biggest of its kind in San Diego police history. He served in World War II and the Korean War as a Marine. He was a marshal in San Diego six years until he was shot in the chest while on duty in 1958.

(Courtesy San Diego Police Museum)

After Bunnell's recovery he could no longer return to law
enforcement. He passed away July 5, 2012 at age 90.

•   Patrolman John Zemcik (1920-1987). World War
II Marine Corps platoon sergeant. He was awarded a
police medal for valor for saving the life of deputy marshal
Elwin Bunnell. (see above) in 1954. Zemcik passed away
in 1987 at age 67.

•   Motorcycle officer Wilfred John "Irish" O'Neal
(1947-1990), Badge 192, 291 & 410. He served 25 years,
retiring in 1972. He passed away from a cerebral
hemorrhage at age 73.

•   San Diego County Superior Court Judge William T.
Low (1922-2004). Early in his judicial career on April 12,
1965, four days after the Hub shootout, Judge Low as a
municipal court judge went to San Diego County Hospital
and presided over Robert Anderson's arraignment at
County Hospital while Anderson was recovering from
gunshot wounds.

(Courtesy San Diego County Judicial Services)
Judge Low was diagnosed with Alzheimer's disease in 2002 and passed away from a heart attack in 2004 at age 82.

•   Inspector Ralph M. Davis, Jr. (1926-2010) Badge #'s 27, 136 & 534. U.S. Army Air Corps World War II and U.S. Air Force Korean War veteran served 28 years with the San Diego Police Department as commanding officer of the Support Services Division. He received a degree in Criminal Justice Administration from Laverne University.

(Courtesy San Diego Police Museum, KGTV and KFMB-TV)

After retiring from the police he was an executive with Dyna Corporation in Carlsbad. He passed away at his Vista home at age 84.

•   San Diego County Superior Court Judge Verne O. Werner passed away on May 6, 1988.

•   Robert L. Thomas (1918-2009) Thomas was the
acting chief deputy district attorney and prosecuted Robert
Anderson.

(Courtesy Brown family)
Thomas, described as "a pillar of the Covenant
Presbyterian Church" in San Diego passed away on
January 15, 2009 and was buried at El Camino Memorial
Park in San Diego. He was 90.
•   San Diego County Deputy District Attorney
Gilbert Smith of La Mesa, one of the prosecutors in Robert
Anderson's murder trial, passed away March 11, 2007.
•   San Diego County Superior Court Judge Robert
Conyers (1917-2011). During World War II he worked as
an FBI special agent investigating domestic espionage
cases. Judge Conyers presided over the second penalty
trial of Robert Anderson.

(Courtesy San Diego County Judicial Services)
He died of pneumonia November 27, 2011 at age 94.
- California Chief Justice, Donald Wright (1907-1985). World War II U.S. Army Air Corps Lieutenant Colonel.

(Courtesy California Supreme Court Historical Society)

In 1972 in People v. Anderson he voted to strike down the death penalty as cruel and unusual punishment and a violation of the state constitution. He passed away at age 78.

•　　　Associate Justice Marshall McComb (1894-1981). Served as an ensign in the U.S. Navy in World War I. He dissented in People v Anderson arguing that the death penalty deterred crime and was so upset about the decision that he walked out of the courtroom.

(Courtesy California Supreme Court Historical Society) In 1977 a panel of Court of Appeal justices forced McComb into retirement by affirming that he had senile dementia and was no longer able to carry out his judicial duties. In 1981 he passed away at age 85 and is buried in Arlington National Cemetery.

•　　　Assistant Police Chief E.C. (Ed) DeBolt (1921-2008) Badge #40. A World War II Army veteran, DeBolt served 30 years with the department and was second in command when he retired.

(Courtesy San Diego Police Museum)
He passed away 45 years and one day after the Hub
shootout at age 86 and was inurned at Fort Rosecrans
National Cemetery.
•   Assistant Police Chief Michael Sgobba (1925-
2011). Sgobba spent 26 years with the department and saw
the formation of the Special Weapons and Tactics
(SWAT) unit.

(Courtesy San Diego Police Museum)
After retiring from the police in 1977 he was appointed by
the Judges of the Municipal Court as Marshal of San
Diego County. He was in that position for 19 years. He

passed away in La Mesa, California in 2011 at age 86 and is buried at Miramar National Cemetery.
* Inspector W.F. Garlington (1926-1978) Badge #17, 45, 95 & 513. His 20-year service on the San Diego Police Department included oversight for the first Special Weapons and Tactics (SWAT) unit, chief of detectives and head of the department's traffic bureau.

(Courtesy San Diego Police Museum)
In 1970 Garlington left San Diego to become chief of police in Vallejo, California. He passed away October 22, 1978 at age 52.
* Deputy Chief William D. Gore (1920-1993) Badge #41. His service to the department began walking an assigned beat and ended 33 years later as third in command.

(Courtesy San Diego Police Museum)
He had the ability to talk to people in a convincing way and became known as the "soft sell man," preferring to talk people into complying with the law. He said he could talk most people into jail than fighting. Gore passed away from Leukemia in 1993 at age 73 and is buried at El Camino Memorial Park in San Diego. Son, Larry was on the police department for 32 years and in 2009 another son, William became San Diego County Sheriff.

Billl Gore
(Courtesy San Diego County Sheriff)

•   Chief Olif J. "Jimmy" Roed (1919-1994). Chief Roed was in command of the department from 1968 to 1971 and served the department 28 years. Chief Roed was an early supporter of the department's use of computers and helicopters.

O.J. Roed 1993
(Courtesy Bob Lampert)

Roed, depressed over health problems, took his own life at his home in 1994. He was 74.

•   Detective Lieutenant Ed Stevens (1927-2014) Badge #30, ID #1919. He joined the Navy in 1944 when he was 17 and in 1950 joined the San Diego Police Department. He excelled as a homicide investigator and even after retirement was called to assist in homicide cases for the San Diego County Sheriff and Escondido Police Department.

Ed Stevens 1995
(Courtesy San Diego Police Museum)
He passed away at home in 2014 at age 86.
•   Assistant Chief Warren Morrison (1914-2004)
Badges 11, 18, 292.

(Courtesy San Diego Police Museum)
Morrison's 32 years with the police department ranged
from being a patrol officer, serving as a police ambulance
driver and paramedic (he delivered 13 babies) to
revamping the police central communications center to
developing the San Diego Police Academy in Mira Mesa.
His life ended in 2004 from a combination of lymphoma,
pneumonia and congestive heart failure. He was 90.

• Chief Ray Hoobler (1927-2001) Badge 81. Hoobler's four years as chief included friction between City Hall and his office.

(Courtesy San Diego Police Museum)

A no-nonsense individualist, Hoobler at 48 stepped down two years before he was old enough to receive a city pension after it was revealed he lied about looking into confidential files of officers who had sought mental counseling. After a struggle with cancer, Hoobler died in 2001 at age 74.

• Captain Tom Hall (1943-2014) Badge #424, ID 1400. Tom Hall served the department for 32 years and then was the chief of police for the San Diego Unified School District.

(Courtesy San Diego Police Museum)
Hall was the officer involved in investigating the 1994
incident when a World War II tank was stolen from a U.S.
National Guard armory in San Diego and was taken on a
rampage through parts of the city. He passed away in 2014
following a long battle with cancer at age 71.

Chapter 20
The Whys and What Ifs

Events change lives. They can be unexpected and happen in a split second. Suddenly one's life moves in a new direction.

There are times we can see life-changing things coming. When they arrive, we can choose to embrace them or turn away. However, in all areas of life, the way we respond and how we use turning points, almost always determines the kind of person we become, and what we pass on to others.

I would not be here if my grandfather on my father's side had not bought another man's passport in Romania and journeyed to America as an illegal immigrant on the cargo ship HMS Carpathia

Once in the United States, he made his way to Minnesota where he was reunited with a girl he knew from Romania. They were married and my father was born in 1915.

What if Grandpa had not been an illegal immigrant?

Fast forward to 1940 when my father met my mother in
Syracuse, New York. She was born in Vienna, Austria and
came with her parents to America. They were married in
1941 and I was born the following year.

 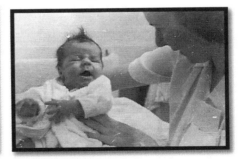

Why was she working at the manufacturing company
where my father got a job?

So far, there are too many "whys and what ifs" for me to know all of this was not coincidental.

Using a line from TV commercials, "But wait, there's more!" On Monday night, December 4, 1972, I received a phone call from a high school classmate, Patti Medaris. People had told her that since I was in television news I didn't have time for my old friends.

She didn't believe it and called me. What if I weren't home that night?

Warp speed ahead. Four days later I asked Patti to marry me. The wedding was in 1973.

Thirteen months later our daughter, Janet was born while Heidi came in 1976.

* * * * *

From a human perspective, this illustrates the unpredictability of life's circumstances but from a Christian understanding, it bolsters a belief that God never takes His eyes off His children.

The Old Testament prophet in Jeremiah 23:24 wrote about God who asks, "Who can hide in secret places that I cannot see them?" That encourages a believer but it also is God's warning.

We can't hide from God or fool Hm. He sees everything people do.

Encouragement is that there is no place where we are beyond the watchful care of our heavenly Father. Even when we feel abandoned and alone, God is with us.

While Christians sometimes can't prevent trials, heartache, or loss, we live with confident faith, knowing an ever-present Creator and Protector watches over our lives and knows in advance why things happen.

Which brings us to what happened at Fifth and F on Thursday, April 8, 1965, an event with and a hundred "whys" and "what ifs."

What if Louis Richards had been ill that day and stayed home?

What if Richards was on vacation?

What if the movie Robert Anderson wanted to see didn't start until 2 P.M.?

Why didn't Anderson pick a different pawnshop?

What if Ted Swienty had been suspicious of Anderson and decided not to show him the rifle?

What if Swienty had telephoned the police a coded "Change Call"?

Why was the window in the room where Swienty hid still blacked out from World War II so Anderson couldn't see him?

What if Robert Crandall had not received the divorce letter that morning from his wife?

Why didn't any bullets fired by police strike Swienty?

What if Swienty had been on the floor over the spot where Sergeant Brown fired his shotgun into the ceiling?

What if a stray bullet had ricocheted into the crowds that were dangerously close?

And the biggest mystery of all: after loading, shooting and reloading his weapons for four hours, why did Robert Anderson put the wrong ammunition in a pistol that misfired twice when he tried to shoot Sergeant Brown?

* * * * *

Two days after the shootout, on April 10, the *San Diego Union* added to the story's "what ifs." The paper wrote about an act of kindness that Hub clerk Ted Swienty did four years earlier that probably saved his life.

Minutes after Anderson shot Richards, Swienty raced upstairs and hid under a bed on the pawnshop's second floor. He remained there while police fired hundreds of rounds of ammunition at Anderson who was barricaded below.

Swienty said the bed was put in a few years earlier out of compassion for night watchman Robert Ramirez who was recovering from cancer surgery. Ramirez wasn't feeling well, so a bed was put on the second floor for him to occasionally rest, an act of kindness greatly appreciated by the ailing night watchman.

In 1964, a year before the shootout, Ramirez died but the bed remained and for Swienty, its presence gave him a place to hide.

"I was grateful for that bed," Swienty said, "even if the springs did touch my chest. That nut with the guns couldn't find me, thank God."

What if the bed were not there?

What if?

Acknowledgements

   This book could not have been completed without the extraordinary help of many people and resources. While appreciation is given to all, a select few are singled out who made major contributions. They include:
•   Steve Willard, retired San Diego Police officer and Vice President of the San Diego Police Museum. Steve was a constant source of encouragement and helped fill in vital pieces of missing information while providing photographs from his excellent book *Images of America San Diego Police Department,* Arcadia Publishing, 2005

•

•   Bob Lampert, retired news photographer, KGTV
San Diego and former reserve police officer.

Bob has an extensive collection of photographs that were
used in the book and also shared his inside information on
the San Diego law enforcement community.
•   Carl Gilman, retired news photographer, KFMB-
TV San Diego and CBS News. Carl's firsthand accounts
helped place the reader on the scene.
•   Frank Brown, retired San Diego Police officer, San
Diego County Deputy District Attorney and Superior
Court Judge. Many delightful hours were spent with Judge
Brown and his wife, Maggie who graciously allowed the
use of photographs of his late father and others at the
shootout scene.

•   Joel Davis, Former Vice President & General
Manager KGTV ABC 10 San Diego and now Vice
President & General Manager WRAL-WRAZ, Raleigh,
North Carolina. KGTV's permission to use photos gleaned
from news film shot April 8, 1965 were invaluable in
writing the book.

(Courtesy KGTV)
•   Dean Elwood, News Director, KFMB-TV. Dean
    was a former colleague of the author's at Channel 8.

(Courtesy KFMB-TV)

The station's approval of using images from news film
shot by Channel 8 April 8-9, 1965 was critical in
combining pictures with words of the events those days.

•   Richard Crawford – writer extraordinaire and supervisor of Special Collections at the San Diego Public Library.

(Courtesy Rick Crawford)

He provided early encouragement for the project and generously shared resources and insight including his story in the *San Diego Union,* July 16, 2009.

Other sources and contributors:

•   AIRCHECK, The Story of Top 40 Radio in San Diego, *San Diego Reader*, Ken Leighton, February 17, 2006.

•   Alex Bell, Group Communications Officer, Public Safety Group, San Diego County.

•   Alicia Fletes, San Diego County Court Operations Supervisor.

•   *All Hands*, October 1965.

•   Alma Cesena, *San Diego Union Tribune* Photo Archives.

•   Alvida Craft, widow of former KOGO-TV/KGTV news photographer, Bob Craft.

•   Amanda Thomas, granddaughter of the late Dave
Crow.
•   Andy Thompson, Poulton-le-Fylde, England
•   Art Farian, retired news photographer, KOGO-
TV/KGTV, San Diego.
•   "Babyface Killers: Horrifying True Stories of
America's Youngest Murderers," Clifford L. Linedecker,
Macmillan, 1999.
•   Ben Cutshall, KFMB-TV news photographer. Ben
was with Channel 8 for 45 years and passed away in 2009
from colon cancer at age 64. Many of his video shots are
shown in this book. He was a master photographer, a
brilliant editor, a superb journalist and a dear friend.

(Courtesy Tom Keck and KFMB-TV)
•   Bob Chandler, retired San Diego radio and TV
sportscaster, writer and former San Diego Padres
announcer.

(Courtesy Bob Chandler)

- Betsy Littrell, KGTV 10 News Assignment Desk.
- Billie Crow, widow of the late Dave Crow.
- *Broadcasting Magazine*, February 18, 1974.
- Carol Meyers, San Diego History Center.
- *Chula Vista Star News*, September 3, 1967.
- Craig Colburn, retired businessman and son of the late Inspector Wayne Colburn.

(Courtesy Craig Colburn)
Craig Colburn sometimes went water skiing with Allen D. Brown and his family, including Brown's son, former Judge Frank Brown.

- *Daily Herald*, Biloxi-Gulfport, Mississippi, March 20, 1972.
- Dave Hall, retired San Diego Police captain, San Diego Harbor Police Chief and original member of the ASP unit.
- Dave Speck, San Diego Police Department SWAT team member.
- David L. McFadden, Board Member, California Supreme Court Historical Society.
- *Desert Sun*, Palm Springs, April 9, 1965.
- Diane Fulham, San Diego County Court Old Records.
- Direct Democracy and the Courts, Kenneth P. Miller, Cambridge University Press, August 31, 2009.
- Gary Gleason, former San Diego Police Department homicide detective, original member of the Anti-Sniper (SWAT) unit and Commander Investigations, San Diego County District Attorney.
- "I Wish I Never Got Off that Bus," Richard A. Serrano, *Los Angeles Times*, April 3, 1990.
- Jack Cavanaugh, author of more than 25 highly acclaimed published novels and a long time friend.

Jack is a great encourager who patiently helped me with manuscript formatting issues.

- Jim Arthur, retired San Diego Police Sergeant and volunteer at San Diego Police Museum.
- Jorge Navarrete, Clerk, California Supreme Court Historical Society.
- "Justice Story: 16-year-old girl shoots up school, tells reporters, 'I Don't Like Mondays,'" Mara Bovsun, *New York Daily News,* November 3, 2013.
- Jutta Biggins, widow of attorney James J. Biggins, Jr. who defended Robert Anderson.
- KFMB-TV news archives, April 8, 1965, https://www.facebook.com/VintageSD/videos/101514055 4524725/
- Karen Dalton, San Diego County Courts, Public Affairs Office, Superior Court of California, County of San Diego.
- Kathy Emmerson, widow of San Diego Police officer Leigh Emmerson.
- KPBS, Ken Kramer's *About San Diego* https://video.kpbs.org/video/ken-kramers-about-san-diego-robert-anderson-shootout-san-diego-police-department-sdpd/.
- Kristi Burns, San Diego Registered Nurse
- Larry Gore, retired San Diego police department commander, member of first Anti-Sniper Platoon and former police chief for West Sacramento, California.
- Larry Morrato, retired San Diego Police Captain who was in charge of security for the 1998 Super Bowl played in San Diego and provided contacts for the book.

(Courtesy S.P.O.A.)

- Lisa Hall, daughter of the late Captain Tom Hall, San Diego Police Department.
- *Long Beach Independent*, April 10, 1968.
- Mel and Mary Knoepp. The retired KFMB-TV Sun Up host and his wife provided insight about the chaos at Fifth and F the day of the shootout.
- Orv Hale, retired San Diego and Carlsbad police officer.
- Our Daily Bread, "Watchful Care," Lisa Samra, July 23, 2018.
- *Pacific Southwest Airlines*, Alan Renga, Mark Mentges, Arcadia Publishing, 2010
- Patrick Vinson, retired San Diego Police Department Sergeant and San Diego Police Museum volunteer. Patrick is an example of the selfless dedication of law enforcement professionals. In July 2018, San Diego Police detective Art Calvert, battling kidney disease, needed a kidney transplant. Vinson was his old supervisor and volunteered to donate his kidney, but it was not a match with Calvert's.

(Courtesy KNSD-TV)

Undeterred, Vinson went ahead and donated his kidney to someone else in Calvert's name and that moved Calvert to the top of a national donor list. End result is that on July 12, 2018, doctors successfully transplanted the kidney of a 30-year-old Colorado man into Calvert. Vinson's kidney was also successfully removed and sent to a different American in need.

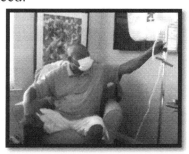

(Courtesy KNSD-TV)

- Proof of Guilt: Barbara Graham and the Politics of Executing Women in America, Kathleen A. Caims, University of Nebraska Press, 2013.
- Raphael Dechief, my IT-savvy son-in-law in Belgium for format solutions.
- Randy Eichman, retired San Diego Police Department Sergeant and San Diego Police Museum volunteer.
- Reid Carroll, retired radio news reporter, XTRA and KFMB San Diego.
- Rick Pace, General Manager, Analog Restaurant/Bar, Fifth and F, San Diego.
- Richard Showalter, retired San Diego police officer 1961-1999.
- Ron Moskowitz, retired San Diego Fire Department Captain, on scene of the shootout as a civilian just before joining the fire department.

(Courtesy Ron Moskowitz)

- *San Bernardino Sun,* April 8, 1965.
- *San Ysidro McDonald Massacre-A Birdseye View* by Monica Zech OB Rag 2004
- Scott Hall, KFMB-TV CBS News 8 Photographer remembers McDonald's massacre, July 18, 2014,

- Sergeant Christopher Sarot, San Diego Police Department Range Master.

Chris Sarot holding the machine gun used by Sergeant Sam Chasteen at the Hub shootout.

- Sharon Chasteen, wife of retired San Diego Police Sergeant, Sam Chasteen.

- Supreme Court of California, In Bank. The PEOPLE, Plaintiff and Respondent, v. Robert Page ANDERSON, Defendant and Appellant. Cr. 9317. Decided: May 24, 1966.

- "Survivor of San Ysidro McDonald's Massacre Shares His Story," City News Service, July 15, 2014.

- Terry Jensen, retired Commander, Bureau of Investigations, San Diego County District Attorney.

Terry has not lost his investigative genius as he solved my most difficult challenges in locating people mentioned in the book.

- Tanya Sierra, Public Affairs Officer, San Diego County District Attorney
- Terry Truitt former San Diego Police Sergeant.
- "The incredible story of the first PC, from 1965," *Tech Musings*, August 28, 2012.
- The Morning Breaks: The Trial of Angela Davis, Bettina Aptheker, Cornell University Press, 1999.
- *The Reader,* "The Seven Wonders of San Diego, The Great Gunfight," Neal Matthews, October 24, 1965.
- *Tucson Daily Citizen,* March 14, 1972, "Story of a Puny Little Man."
- Virginia Creighton, KGTV 10 News Assignment Desk.

Made in the USA
Middletown, DE
03 November 2018